# GROWTH AND RECOVERY PERFORMANCE OF LEAD BANK

# GROWTH AND RECOVERY PERFORMANCE OF LEAD BANK


***By***

**Dr. I. Sheeja**

*Research Scholar*

*PG & Research Centre in Commerce*

*Scott Christian College (Autonomous)*

*Nagercoil*

*Kanyakumari District*

*Tamilnadu*

*(INDIA)*

*&*

**Dr. X.Antony Thanaraj**

*Associate Professor*

*PG & Research Centre in Commerce*

*Scott Christian College (Autonomous)*

*Nagercoil*

*Kanyakumari district*

*Tamilnadu*

*(INDIA)*

**DISCOVERY PUBLISHING HOUSE PVT. LTD.**

**NEW DELHI-110 002**

*Published by:*
**Tilak Wasan**

**DISCOVERY PUBLISHING HOUSE PVT. LTD.**
4383/4B, Ansari Road, Darya Ganj
New Delhi-110 002 (India)
*Phone* : +91-11-23279245, 43596064-65
*Fax* : +91-11-23253475
*E-mail* : parul.wasan@gmail.com
discoverypublishinghouse@gmail.com
*web* : www.discoverypublishinggroup.com

*First Edition:* **2012**

**ISBN: 978-93-5056-088-4**

**Growth and Recovery Performance of Lead Bank**



***Printed at:***
***Shree Balaji Art Press***
***Delhi***

# Preface

The banking sector has a crucial role to play in all economic and commercial pursuits. It serves as the engine of growth and development. The very morphology and functional desiderata of the banking sector have been undergoing changes for the better, consistently and continuously over the years. A number of novel and innovative schemes and programmes have been designed and implemented. Among them, the Lead Bank Scheme (LBS) of 1969 plays a strategic role in the Indian economy.

The Lead bank is expected to assume a major role in the development of banking and credit in the allotted districts. It will primarily be responsible for surveying the credit needs, developing a network of branches and extending adequate credit facilities through the co-operation of other banks operating in the district. The Lead bank is also expected to maintain contacts and liaison with government and quasi-government agencies engaged in development activities. In other words, the lead bank is expected to promote all round development of the allotted district. It is, however, to be noted that the lead bank is not expected to have a monopoly of banking business in a district.

This book has covered all the major segments of the subject and is divided into seven chapters spread over the following topics:

Introduction and Design of the Study;

Review of Literature;

Functions and Organisational Structure of Lead Bank;

Trend and Growth of Lead Bank Schemes;

Evaluation of Lead Bank Schemes — Block-wise Comparison of Growth and Equity;

Impact of Government Sponsored Programmes under the Lead Bank Scheme on Income, Asset, Employment Generation and Recovery Performance; and

Summary of Findings, Suggestions and Conclusion.

I hope it would serve as a useful text and reference book for all categories of readers, particularly academics, researchers, practitioners and government agencies.

Any constructive criticism and suggestion is always welcome.

**Dr. I. Sheeja**
**Dr. X. Antony Thanaraj**

# Contents

# 1

# Introduction and Design of the Study

## INTRODUCTION

India's economy is agrarian, planned, mixed and developing in character. The Five Year Plans (FYP) and the recent Structural Adjustment Programmes (SAP) and the Economic Reforms involving Liberalization, Globalization and Privatization (LGP) have, successfully, been transforming the social, economic and commercial aspects of India. Though agriculture and industries enjoy the primary and secondary sector status conditions, the tertiary or services-sector, functions as the bedrock on which all the others hinge and thrive. Transportation, banking, power, education, health and trade are the strong pillars of this vital branch of the economy.

The banking sector has a crucial role to play in all economic and commercial pursuits. It serves as the engine of growth and development. The very morphology and functional desiderata of the banking sector have been undergoing changes for the better, consistently and continuously over the years. A number of novel and innovative schemes and programmes have been designed and implemented. Among them, the Lead Bank Scheme (LBS) of 1969 plays a strategic role in the Indian economy.

A notable feature of Indian Commercial Banks, prior to the introduction of social control over banks in 1969 and nationalization of the 14 major banks on July 19, 1969, was that majority of the banks were controlled by leaders of commerce and industry. At the end of March 1951, 36 per cent of the bank credit was absorbed by trade and 34 per cent by industry and at the end of March 1956, the share of industry and commerce in the total bank credit continued to be 37.10 per cent and 36.50 per cent respectively. The beneficiaries of the bank credit were the people connected with the administration of banks.

The National Credit Council (NCC) was set up in February 1968, with a view to providing a forum for discussion and appraisal of credit priorities on an all India basis. The following were the leading periodical functions of the NCC:

*(a)* To assess the demand for bank credit from the various sectors of the economy;

*(b)* To determine priorities for grant of loans and advances, or for investment, having regard to the availability of resources and requirements of the priority sector in particular, such as agriculture, small scale industries and exports; and

*(c)* To co-ordinate lending and investment policies among the commercial and co-operative banks and specialised agencies to ensure optimum utilization of resources.

Although the banking system has taken certain steps for achieving the objectives of social control, the progress made in this regard was not adequate. With a view to ensuring that the banks were adequately motivated towards a speedy achievement of the social purposes like meeting the legitimate requirements of the weaker sections of the society, 14 major commercial banks were nationalized on July 19, 1969.

In a country, where a large segment of population is wallowing in poverty, social needs and expectations cannot be ignored and the public sector banking system will need to reorient its functioning, in a way, which makes it an effective instrument of service to the community. Interest mechanism should sub-serve the objective of social justice in the matter of distribution of credit but at the same time, the banks should continue to retain their character as viable institutions.

The extension of credit to small borrowers in priority sector is the prime aim of nationalization and therefore, its magnitude is the real test of its success.

As of now, the Government has classified the weaker sections of borrowers as follows:

- People who have really no tangible security of any worth to offer on their own;
- Cannot produce a security/guarantee of a well-to-do party;
- Are prepared to work hard;
- Can be helped to rise above their present economic levels in a productive endeavour with assistance from banks, the productive endeavour being such as would become economically viable within a period of about 3 years; and
- Do not incur liability to two sources of finance at the same time.

The following are among the sectors, within which the banks could locate parties who deserve the differential rates:

- Scheduled tribes, scheduled castes and others engaged in a very modest scale in agriculture;
- People who themselves collect or do elementary processing of forest products and people who themselves collect fodder in difficult areas and sell them to farmers or traders;
- People, physically engaged on a modest scale, in the fields of cottage and rural industries and vocations in urban

areas. Illustrative examples are: cutting cloth and sewing garments, making reasonably cheap eatables, home delivery service of articles and commodities of daily use, running way-side tea-stalls, plying of self-owned manual rickshaws and cycle-rickshaws, repairing shoes, sandals, basket-making mainly by hand, etc.;

- Intelligent students who prosecute their higher education but do not get scholarships/maintenance grants, from government or educational authorities;
- Physically challenged persons, pursuing a gainful occupation, where some durable equipment and/ continuous supply of raw material is necessary;
- Orphanages and women's homes, where saleable goods are made and for which no adequate and dependable sources of finance like endowment or regular charities exist.

In a fitting message to the International Seminar on Banking and Development, the Prime Minister observed: "Economic growth is important for all countries. For the poorer countries it is vital. Of the many structural and institutional changes that are necessary in developing countries, not the least important is the adaptation of financial institutions to serve the objectives of development and bring about greater mobility of resources, to meet the emerging needs of the economy". In India, we have taken several steps designed to make our banking system, development-oriented and to set up special institutions to give the requisite financial support to the new development in industry and agriculture, to large-scale industry and small-scale entrepreneurs. Our concern has been not only with growth but also with ensuring that the benefits of development reach out more and more to the vast masses of population. The stress was on the 'trackle down' effect.

## LEAD BANK SCHEME (LBS)

The Lead Bank Scheme was evolved in 1969 as an important organisational framework to fulfill the objective of increasing bank finance to priority sector and also to promote their role in the overall development of the various districts in the country. All districts have been allocated to various banks, designated as the Lead Banks for the districts[1]. Indian Overseas Bank (IOB) is the Lead Bank for Kanyakumari District.

The Lead Bank Scheme has been based on the 'area approach' to banking. Its prime goal is to achieve 100 per cent balanced distribution of bank branches among the several towns and villages in a district. The sofar unbanked or underbanked areas, particularly, in rural areas, will be brought into the network of banks[2].

The function of the Lead Bank is to co-ordinate the efforts of all other banks, financial institutions and other development agencies, such as District Rural Development Agencies, District Industries Centres, Backward Classes Corporations, and Housing Development Authorities/Boards, working at various levels, for bringing about the overall development of the districts.

The scheme now covers 526 districts in the country[3]. Annual Credit Plans (ACPs) are prepared on the deployment of credit for numerous activities and the progress in implementation thereof is reviewed in meetings of Block Level Bankers Committees (BLBCs), District Consultative Committees (DCCs) and State Level Bankers' Committees (SLBCs). The Reserve Bank of India monitors the progress, in the implementation of Annual Credit Plans through its Regional Offices.

## SERVICE AREA APPROACH (SAA)

With the establishment of the wide network of bank branches in rural and semi-urban areas in the late eighties, studies were undertaken to assess the impact of bank credit in increasing production, productivity and income levels of the rural population. These studies revealed several weaknesses in the existing system of dispensation of rural credit namely rural lending by bank branches was rather haphazard and dispersed in a large number of villages spread over a wide area, rendering supervision difficult. It was therefore felt that a move should be made towards concentrated lending, by adopting an approach of designating specific service areas to the bank branches in rural and semi-urban areas in which they can operate for productive lending. It was felt that such an approach had significant advantages in contributing to orderly and planned development of the entire identified area and in monitoring and supervising credit and ensuring better recovery. Besides assessment of the impact of bank credit on production, productivity and income levels, it would also help in harmonising the efforts of banks in the task of rural development and avoiding diffusion of efforts over wide areas.

A decentralised planning policy was adopted and the Service Area Approach (SAA) was introduced in April 1989. Accordingly, each rural and semi-urban branch was allotted a specific area comprising of 15 to 25 villages, based on the principles of contiguity and proximity and it was asked to prepare an Annual Credit Plan on Service Area Plan after careful assessment of the potentialities and the needs of the various priority sector activities in its service area[4]. Annual Lending Programmes, drawn up by all branches in the Block/Taluk, were thereafter aggregated to form the Block Credit Plan (BCP) for the block, as a whole, and the District Credit Plan (DCP) was prepared by aggregation of all Block Credit Plans in the district.

The implementation of BCPs was reviewed at Block Level Bankers' Committee, convened every quarter. Lead District Officers (LDOs) of the Reserve Bank of India attended these meetings selectively, in order to monitor the progress under District Credit Plans and various other programmes. Service Area Monitoring and Information System (SAMIS) were introduced as a medium for reporting the progress in the Lead Bank Returns (LBR) through which the Reserve Bank of India, in association with National Bank for Agriculture and

Rural Development, monitors its usefulness and effectiveness. Under SAMIS, code numbers were allocated to each activity and the information is suitably computerised[5].

Table 1.1 shows the Number of Districts in Tamil Nadu and the Lead Banks in the Respective Districts

**Table 1.1: Names of the Lead Banks in Tamil Nadu (District-wise)**

| Sl. No. | District | Name of the Lead Bank |
|---|---|---|
| (1) | (2) | (3) |
| 1. | Ariaylur | State Bank of India |
| 2. | Chennai | State Bank of India |
| 3. | Coimbatore | Canara Bank |
| 4. | Cuddalore | Indian Bank |
| 5. | Dharmapuri | Indian Bank |
| 6. | Dindigul | Canara Bank |
| 7. | Erode | Canara Bank |
| 8. | Kancheepuram | Indian Overseas Bank |
| 9. | Kanyakumari | Indian Overseas Bank |
| 10. | Karur | Indian Overseas Bank |
| 11. | Madurai | Canara Bank |
| 12. | Nagapattinam | Indian Overseas Bank |
| 13. | Namakkal | Indian Overseas Bank |
| 14. | Nilgiris | Canara Bank |
| 15. | Perambalur | Indian Bank |
| 16. | Pudukkottai | Indian Overseas Bank |
| 17. | Ramanathapuram | Indian Overseas Bank |
| 18. | Salem | Indian Bank |
| 19. | Sivaganga | Indian Overseas Bank |
| 20. | Thanjavur | Indian Overseas Bank |
| 21. | Theni | Canara Bank |
| 22. | Thiruvallur | Indian Bank |

*(Contd...)*

| (1) | (2) | (3) |
|---|---|---|
| 23. | Thiruvarur | Indian Overseas Bank |
| 24. | Tiruchirapalli | Indian Overseas Bank |
| 25. | Tirunelveli | Indian Overseas Bank |
| 26. | Tiruvannamalai | Indian Bank |
| 27. | Thoothukudi | State Bank of India |
| 28. | Vellore | Indian Bank |
| 29. | Villupuram | Indian Bank |
| 30. | Virudhunagar | Indian Overseas Bank |

*Source:* National Bank for Agriculture and Rural Development, Chennai

As per the above table there are 30 districts in Tamil Nadu and four nationalized banks are playing the role of Lead Bank. Indian Overseas Bank is the Lead Bank for 13 districts, followed by Indian Bank for eight districts, Canara Bank and State Bank of India for six and three districts respectively.

## GOVERNMENT-SPONSORED EMPLOYMENT SCHEMES

The Government of India had initiated Integrated Rural Development Programme (IRDP) and Development of Women and Children in Rural Areas (DWCRA) for reaching the poor with credit facilities. Later, it was found that these programmes failed to reach the needy due to various reasons. Therefore, the Government launched some other programmes namely Prime Minister Rozgar Yojana (PMRY), Swarnajayanthi Gram Swarozger Yojana (SGSY), Swarna Jayanthi Shahari Rozgar Yojana (SJSRY) and Tamilnadu AdhiDravida Housing Development Corporation (TAHDCO) and other schemes to ameliorate the lot of the poor, through self-employment activities[6].

Leading employment schemes are presented in this section. These programmes are implemented through various commercial banks. Indian Overseas Bank, which is the lead bank in Kanyakumari district, prepares the Annual Credit Plan and co-ordinates the activities of the commercial banks.

## The Prime Minister's Rozgar Yojana (PMRY)

The performance of any viable scheme is based on certain guidelines. The implementing agencies could perform their functions only based on guidelines. The guidelines are self-explanatory so that various District Industries Centres and Banks, located all over India, can implement several schemes in a uniform manner. The recently announced PMRY scheme has certain well-defined guidelines. The Reserve Bank of India announced a new loan scheme, formulated by the Government of India called PMRY, for the educated unemployed youth which was launched on 2nd October 1993.The objective of the scheme is to provide employment to more than a million persons by setting up 7 lakhs micro-enterprises for and by the educated unemployed youth. These micro enterprises will cover manufacturing (industries) services and business ventures. The salient features of the scheme are as follows:[7]

### Target Group

The scheme covers all educated unemployed youth, who have done matriculation (passed or failed). Preference is given to ITI passed women and to persons who have completed the government-sponsored technical course for a minimum duration of 6 months and fulfilling the following conditions:

- The applicant should be within the age group of 18 to 35 years;
- The total annual family income of the applicant should not exceed Rs. 24,000;
- The term 'family' for this purpose, would mean spouse and parents of the beneficiary and 'family income' would include income from all sources, like wages, salary, pension, agriculture, business and rent. A defaulter to a bank/financial institution will not be eligible for assistance under the scheme. More than one member of the same family will not get assistance under this scheme. If, however, a member of the family is the defaulter to a bank/financial institution, other members of the same family will not be eligible for assistance under this scheme;

- The beneficiary should be a permanent resident of the area continuously for three years. Documents like the ration card will constitute enough proof for this purpose. In its absence, residency certificate issued by the Deputy Commissioner/District Magistrate or any other appropriate authority, designated by the State government may be taken;
- The applicant should have the necessary skill in the proposed venture and aptitude for undertaking the activity;
- The applicant should not have borrowed from any bank/ credit institution under similar schemes of the government of India, state government or state-owned corporation for the assistance to the poorer sections of the society.

**The Million Wells Scheme (MWS)**

The Million Wells Scheme (MWS) has been implemented as a separate scheme with effect from 1st January 1996. The objective is to argument, the irrigation potential and assist in the development of the lands of the marginal farmers, belonging to SC/ST and freed bonded labour. The scheme is 100 per cent subsidized. Later, this scheme became available to non-SC/ST beneficiaries also provided they fulfill the other conditions.

**Ganga Kalyan Yojana (GKY)**

The Ganga Kalyan Yojana (GKY) is another poverty alleviation scheme. It was launched on 1st February 1997. It seeks to provide irrigation facilities through ground water sources to small and marginal farmers, below poverty line.

**Swarna Jayanthi Shahari Rozgar Yojana (SJSRY)**

With a view to rationalising the different urban poverty alleviation programmes, the Swarna Jayanthi Shahari Rozgar Yojana was launched in December 1977. (This scheme replaced then existing schemes namely, Scheme of Urban Micro

Enterprises and Prime Minister's Urban Poverty Eradication Programme). This scheme which is operative in all urban areas has the following two components:

1. The Urban Self Employment Programme (USEP);
2. The Urban Wage Employment Programme (UWEP).

The target group for the programme is the urban poor, defined as those living below the poverty line (BPL). While identifying beneficiaries, women belonging to women-headed households would be ranked higher than others. Preference is given to Scheduled Castes/Scheduled Tribes and disabled persons. Under the scheme, projects upto a maximum unit cost of Rs. 50,000 will be financed by banks and subsidy is available from the Government upto 15 per cent of the project cost, while the beneficiary is required to contribute 5 per cent of project cost as margin money. Group endeavours are also eligible for financial assistance. Banks are not to insist on collateral security[8].

The Government would provide training and other support services. This scheme also grants special incentives to urban poor women, who decide to set up self employment ventures as a group. Its objective is community empowerment through promoting community organisation like the Neighbourhood Groups (NHGs), the Neighbourhood Committees (NHCs), and the Community Development Societies (CDSs). The CDS will be the nodal agency for project identification and coordination[9].

## Swarnajayanthi Gram Swarozgar Yojana (SGSY)

The SGSY is a self-employment programme, launched with effect from April 1, 1999. This programme is a revamp of the erstwhile Integrated Rural Development Programme (IRDP), Development for Woman and Children in Rural Areas (DWCRA), Training of Rural Youth for Self-Employment (TRYSEM), Supply of Improved Toolkits to Rural Artisans (SITRA), Ganga Kalyan Yojana (GKY) and Million Wells Scheme (MWS). It must be pointed out that SGSY has been devised, keeping in view the positive aspects and deficiencies of the earlier programmes. The earlier programmes were originally viewed as complementary to each other to achieve the large goal of poverty alleviation. But over the years, each one of these, started operating almost as a separate and independent programme. Obviously, the concern was more for achieving individual progaramme targets. The desired linkages among the programmes and the much-needed focus on the substantive issue of sustainable income generation were missing. The SGSY, accordingly, came into being after restructuring all these programmes.

The SGSY has a definite objective of improving the family income of the rural poor and at the same time, providing for the flexibility of design at the grassroot level, to suit the local needs and resources. The objective of the restructuring was to make the programme more effective in providing a sustainable income through micro-enterprise development, both land based and otherwise. In doing so, effective linkages have been established between various components such as capacity, building of the poor, particularly, rural women, credit, technology, marketing and infrastructure.

The salient features of the SGSY are as follows:

- It aims at establishing a large number of micro enterprises in the rural areas, building upon the potential of the rural poor;
- The assisted families (known as swarozgaris) may be individuals or groups (self help groups of SHGs). Emphasis is, however, on the group approach;
- In establishing the micro-enterprises, 4-5 key activities are to be identified in each block, based on the resources, occupational skills of the people and availability of markets. The major share of SGSY assistance will be an activity cluster;
- SGSY adopts a project approach for each key activity. Project reports are to be prepared, in respect of identified key activities. The banks and other financial institutions

are closely associated with and involved in preparing their project reports, so as to avoid delays in the sanctioning of loans and to ensure adequacy of financing;

- The existing infrastructure for the cluster of activities is reviewed and the gaps identified. Critical gaps in investment are made under SGSY, subject to a ceiling of 20 per cent (25 per cent in the case of north-eastern states) of the total programme's allocation for each district. This amount is maintained by the District Rural Development Agencies (DRDAs) as 'SGSY Infrastructure Fund' and it can also be utilised to generate additional funding from other sources;
- SGSY is a credit-cum-subsidy programme. However, credit is the critical component in SGSY, subsidy being only a minor and enabling element. Accordingly, SGSY envisages a greater involvement of the banks;
- It seeks to promote multiple credits rather than a one time credit 'injection';
- Emphasis is to be laid on skill development through well designed training courses;
- SGSY ensures upgradation of the technology, in the identified activity clusters;
- It provides for promotion of marketing of the goods produced by the SGSY swarozgaris. This involves provision of market intelligence, development of markets, consultancy services as well as institutional arrangements for the marketing of the goods including exports;
- Subsidy under SGSY is uniform at 30 per cent of the project cost, subject to a maximum of Rs. 7,500. It is 50 per cent and Rs. 10,000 for SCs/STs but 50 per cent of the cost of the scheme, subject to a ceiling of Rs. 1.25 lakhs for the Swarozgaris. There is no monetary limit on subsidy for irrigation projects. Subsidy will be back ended[10].

- SGSY has a special focus on the vulnerable groups among the rural poor. Accordingly, the SC/ST would amount for at least 50 per cent of the Swarozgaris, women accounting for 40 per cent and the differently abled 3 per cent;
- The programme is implemented by the DRDAs through the Panchayat Samitis. The process of planning, implementation and monitoring integrates the banks and other financial institutions, in the district. DRDAs are being suitably revamped and strengthened;
- Fifteen per cent of the funds, under the SGSY are set apart for the national-level projects of far-reaching significance and which can also act as indicators of possible alternative strategies to be taken up in conjunction with the other departments or semi-government and international organisation. This includes initiatives to be taken up in the individual district or across the districts;
- Funds under SGSY are shared by the Central and State Governments in the ratio of 75 : 25;
- The central allocation, earmarked for the state, is distributed in relation to the incidence of poverty in the states. However, additional parameters like absorption capacity and special requirements will also be taken into consideration during the course of the year[11].

## Self-Help Groups through Swarnajayanthi Gram Swarozgar Yojana (SGSY)

The success of Self Help Groups (SHGs) formed by Non Governmental Organisations (NGOs) in facilitating the flow of credit in rural areas and ensuring nearly 95 to 97 per cent repayment, has resulted in it being considered as the remedy for all the ills faced by the rural poor. Poverty alleviation, which was an intrinsic component of SHGs had acquired prominence in government circles because there were a number of development initiatives and schemes for the generation of self-employment in rural areas for many decades.

The reorganized self-employment programme, that is SGSY, is the outcome of the experience gained from programmes such as IRDP, TRYSEM, DWCRA, SITRA and MWS. It is an innovative programme to promote people living below the poverty line and to promote the establishment of micro enterprises in rural areas, which ought to yield a monthly income of Rs. 2000 per family within three years.

The SGSY and SHG may each consist of 10 or 20 persons but only one member from a family can avail financial assistance from SGSY, of which 75 per cent would be in the form of group loans. Defaulters are excluded from the scheme. The scheme lays emphasis on two important aspects, namely, group enterprise and key activity. Every aspect of enterprise promotion, namely, credit, subsidy, skill training, management training, key activity technology and marketing is taken care of. The programme takes care of the problems of women.

The group has a code of conduct and conducts meetings regularly (weekly or fortnightly), in a democratic manner, allowing free exchange of views and participation by the members in the decision-making process.

The group gives priorities to the loan applications, fixes repayment schedule, fixes appropriate rate of interest for the loans advanced and closely monitors the repayment of loan installment.

The SHG will be an informal group. The groups can also register themselves under the Societies Registration Act, the State Co-operative Act or as a partnership firm. The SHGs can be further strengthened and stabilized by federating them at, say, village level[12].

## Tamil Nadu Adhidravida Housing Development Corporation (TAHDCO) Land Purchase Scheme

Components of the scheme:

- Purchase of land
- Development of land
- Minor irrigation facilities

- Animal Husbandry Activities
- Electricity service connections on priority
- Cash credit for crop loan
- Comprehensive input assistance from agriculture, horticulture, animal husbandry and other departments
- Partial exemption from Stamp Duty and Registration charges

**Purchase of Land**

Each beneficiary under this scheme can own upto 5 acres of dry land or 2.50 acres of wet land including the land, if any, already owned by himself and his family members.

**Development of Land**

Land development activities, such as land clearance, land leveling, shaping and construction of shoulder bunds can be undertaken under this component.

**Minor Irrigation**

Financial assistance will be extended for erecting bore wells, open wells, filter points, electric motors, oil engines/ submersible pumpsets in well bores, shallow tube wells, dug cum bore wells, drip irrigation, sprinkler irrigation and pipe lines. Beneficiaries can also undertake any activity allied to agriculture.

**Electricity Service Connection on Priority**

Tamil Nadu Electricity Board will provide electricity service connection on priority loan's for agriculture pump sets, to the beneficiaries availing assistance under this scheme, within 3 months from the date of application. For every service connection provided by TNEB, under this scheme, TAHDCO will provide Rs. 10,000 to TNEB, from the infrastructure fund provided under Special Capital Assistance. No charges will be levied by TNEB from the beneficiaries for such priority service connections.

## Cash Credit Under Crop Loan Scheme

Beneficiaries under this scheme can avail crop loan, from the Primary Agricultural Co-operative Societies (PACS) and Commercial Banks. The scale of finance for different crops will be as determined by the State Level Committee for the particular year.

## Comprehensive Input Assistance from Agriculture, Horticulture, Animal Husbandry Departments

Beneficiaries under this scheme will be provided comprehensive escort service by agriculture, horticulture and animal husbandry departments, in the form of customized training, extension services and all other inputs, provided under the ongoing schemes of the departments, as per the requirements of the beneficiaries.

## Partial Exemption from Stamp Duty and Registration Charges

Exemption to the extent of 75 per cent of the amount chargeable under stamp duty and registration fees is be provided for beneficiaries and 25 per cent of this amount is borne by the beneficiaries, as part of the project loan.

## Scale of Finance

The scales of finance for various components are as follows:

- Purchase of Land Rs. 1, 00,000 (Maximum)
- ❖ Land development
  - ❖ Minor irrigation Rs. 1,00,000 (Maximum)
  - ❖ Animal Husbandry, Allied activities such as dairy and poultry farming.

Each beneficiary is eligible to avail finance for all the components of the scheme, as listed above, or any one of the components or a combination of one or more components of the scheme.

For the purpose of valuation of the land, for fixing the quantum of finance, the guideline value fixed by the registration department, for the particular piece of land, or the market price, whichever is lower, will be made applicable. The maximum quantum of finance for purchase of land is Rs. 1,00,000 only.

As regards the unit cost for land development, minor irrigation and animal husbandry and allied activities, the unit cost norms prescribed by NABARD, for such activities, will be applicable for the purpose of fixing the quantum of finance. The maximum quantum permitted for each such activity is Rs. 1,00,000 only.

### Subsidy

The pattern of financial assistance will be 50 per cent subsidy and 50 per cent as term loan. The subsidy will be back ended.

### Eligibility

The beneficiaries should be Scheduled Caste/Scheduled Tribe women between 18 and 55 years of age. Land will be registered in the name of woman beneficiaries only.

The beneficiaries can be landless agricultural labourers or tenant farmers or sharecroppers or small/marginal farmers but priority given to the landless agricultural labourers. Two-thirds of the annual target will be earmarked for landless agricultural labourers/tillers and one-third will be earmarked for marginal farmers/small farmers.

The beneficiary should be below the poverty line (BPL).

Only one beneficiary from a family will be eligible to avail assistance from the scheme.

Maximum coverage of beneficiaries will be from Scheduled Caste and Scheduled Tribe women members of Self Help Groups (SHGs).

### Selection Procedure

The District Selection Committee shall select the beneficiaries according to the eligibility of the individual and viability of the project.

## General Guidelines

The land to be purchased should be selected by the beneficiaries themselves. The decision to purchase and sell land rests only on the buyer and seller of the land respectively.

The land purchased under this scheme should not be sold within 10 years or during the period of loan, whichever is lower.

The maximum scale of finance of Rs. 2 lakhs does not include crop loan.

## Rural Employment Generation Programme (Gramodyog Rozgar) By Khadi and Village Industries Commission (KVIC)

Rural Employment Generation Programme (REGP) is implemented by Khadi and Village Industries Commission (KVIC) with an objective to provide employment in rural areas and development of entrepreneurial skill among the rural unemployed youth for achieving the goal of rural industrialisation. There are about 119 village industries under the purview of KVIC, for getting the margin financial assistance. The investment ceiling is Rs. 25 lakhs. KVIC will provide 25 per cent of the project cost upto Rs. 10 lakhs as margin money whereas for projects above Rs. 10 lakhs and upto Rs. 25 lakhs, the rate of margin money will be 25 per cent of the project cost upto Rs.10 lakhs plus 10 per cent of the remaining cost of the project. In the case of weaker sections, the margin money will be 30 per cent of the project cost upto Rs. 10 lakhs and for the project which costs above Rs. 10 lakhs, an additional 10 per cent will be given. The maximum amount of margin money admissible is Rs. 2.5 lakhs for general category and Rs. 3 lakhs for weaker sections, irrespective of the project cost. The bank will sanction 90 per cent of the project cost as loan in case of general category and 95 per cent of the project cost in the case of weaker sections. The unit to be financed under REGP of KVIC should be registered with KVIC and a certificate of registration should be obtained. Individuals/Institutions/Co-operative societies/Trusts/SHGs can avail of the benefits under the scheme[13].

## New Anna Marumalarchi Thittam—2002

The Tamil Nadu Government has announced the New Anna Marumalarchi Thittam, for establishing agro based/food processing industries in each block of the State. Under the scheme, projects of Rs. 20 lakhs and above from individuals, firms, limited companies and projects of Rs. 5 lakhs and above from Self Help Groups will be considered. The promoter should contribute 20 per cent of the loan amount as margin and 50 per cent to other collateral security. The following incentives are available under the scheme:[14]

- Special capital incentive scheme which provides 15 per cent as subsidy, on investment in plant and machinery, limited to Rs. 15 lakhs per block[15].
- The unit set up under this scheme will be entitled to Low Tension Power Tariff subsidy (LTPT) of 30 per cent, 20 per cent and 10 per cent of energy charges in the first, second and third year respectively, from the date of commencement of production or date of power connection whichever is later[16].
- The units set up under this scheme will be eligible for generator subsidy of 15 per cent of the cost of the generator, with the maximum of Rs. 5 lakhs.
- If women constitute more than 50 per cent of the work force of a unit, it will be eligible for an additional 5 per cent capital subsidy, subject to a limit of Rs. 5 lakhs.

## TREND IN BANK ADVANCES

The amount of bank advance in Tamil Nadu has increased from Rs. 380.63 crores in June 1969 to Rs. 6, 537.44 crores in June 1987. A break-up of the overall growth shows that advances in rural areas formed only 1.2 per cent of the total bank advances at the end of June 1969. This increased to 12.2 per cent by the end of June 1987. The advances in semi-urban areas constituted only 13.4 per cent of the total in June 1989, which increased to 18.6 per cent in June 1987. The advances in urban metropolitan areas, declined from 85.4 per cent in

June 1969 to 69.2 per cent in June 1987. Thus, advances continued to increase, but faster in rural and semi-urban areas. It is evident, that since the nationalisation of major banks in 1969, emphasis has positively been shifted to rural and semi-urban areas from urban/metropolitan centres. In other words, there has been an increase in the financial assistance from banks to agriculture and allied activities, activities in priority and neglected sectors, during this period.

**Table 1.2: Extent of Advances Made in Tamil Nadu**

**(*Rs. in Crores*)**

| Sl. No. | Region | Advances | | | |
|---|---|---|---|---|---|
| | | 1980-81 | 1990-91 | 2000-01 | 2008-09 |
| 1. | Rural | 189.21 | 1452.14 | 4093.35 | 9382.00 |
| 2. | Semi-Urban | 373.08 | 1926.15 | 6122.91 | 14752.00 |
| 3. | Urban | 1460.93 | 8207.82 | 40065.48 | 86671.00 |
| | **Total** | **2023.22** | **11586.11** | **50281.74** | **11085.00** |

*Source:* Tamil Nadu—An Economic Appraisal, Directorate of Evaluation and Applied Research, Tamil Nadu, 2008-2009.

In the aggregate, the quantum of advances made moved up from Rs. 2023.22 crores in 1980-81 to Rs. 11586.11 crores in 1990-91 and further to Rs. 50281.74 crores in 2000-01. It stood at Rs. 11085 crores in 2008-09. The aggregate advances made by commercial banks increased over the years in all the three regions. The advances stood at Rs. 9382 crores for rural areas, Rs. 14752 crores for semi-urban areas and Rs. 86671 crores for urban areas during 2008-09.

Regarding credit by each bank branch in Tamil Nadu, it was Rs. 45.68 crores in urban areas, Rs. 11.54 crores in semi-urban areas and Rs. 5.42 crores in rural areas in the year 2008-09, whereas India, it was Rs. 44.20 crores in urban areas, Rs. 8.62 crores in semi-urban areas and Rs. 3.47 crores in rural areas in 2008-09. This table drives home the point, that credit off-take is also heavily skewed towards urban areas.

**Table 1.3: Advances by Each Bank Branch in India and Tamil Nadu**

(*Rs. in Crores*)

| Sl. No. | Area | 2005-06 | | 2006-07 | | 2007-08 | | 2008-09 | |
|---|---|---|---|---|---|---|---|---|---|
| | | Tamil Nadu | All India | Tamil Nadu | All India | Tamil Nadu | All India | Tamil Nadu | All India |
| 1. | Rural | 2.62 | 2.02 | 3.17 | 2.33 | 3.92 | 2.69 | 5.42 | 3.47 |
| 2. | Semi-Urban | 6.25 | 4.84 | 7.33 | 5.60 | 8.83 | 6.69 | 11.54 | 8.62 |
| 3. | Urban | 28.45 | 27.24 | 33.77 | 29.65 | 38.81 | 34.86 | 45.68 | 44.20 |

*Source:* Tamil Nadu—An Economic Appraisal, Directorate of Evaluation and Applied Research, Chennai, 2008-2009.

## CREDIT DEPOSIT RATIO

The ratio of credit to deposits, is an important indicator of the absorptive capacity of a region on one hand and the level of response on the other. Regarding Tamil Nadu as a whole, the credit-deposit ratio has moved to 103 per cent at the end of June 1990. The national average also declined from 77.00 per cent at the end of June 1969 to 66 per cent at the end of June 1990. The main reason for the decline in the credit-deposit ratio is the increase in the statutory liquidity ratio and cash reserve ratio. But Tamil Nadu as a whole, had a higher credit - deposit ratio than the national average, which clearly indicates an inflow of bank funds to the state from other parts of the country, for lending purposes. The credit-deposit ratio for the rural sector has increased from 62.6 per cent in June 1969 to 93.8 per cent in June 1987, indicating an increase in the flow of funds to rural areas for financing agriculture and allied activities. Both in semi-urban and urban/metropolitian areas, the ratios through declined, were well above national averages. The banks in Tamil Nadu have maintained advance portfolio well above the national level[17].

As the state economy is improving, the outlook for banking performance is good. The economic growth rate in Tamil Nadu during 1985-86 was impressive, measured in terms of state domestic product, it stood at 11.40 per cent. In the following year 1986-87, the targeted growth rate of 5 per cent was almost achieved, which instilled great confidence among the people in monetary circles. However, difficult challenges lie ahead. Commercial banks have been directed to finance the expansion of priority sectors and weaker sections of the society at lower interest rates. The banks in Tamil Nadu would be able to weather any economic storm by prudent management of their deposits and other working funds[18].

The Table 1.4 highlights the fact that the credit-deposit ratio is higher in Tamil Nadu than that at the all India level. The ratio works out to 90 per cent and above in the recent past consecutively. It was 103 per cent during the year 1989-1990 and for the year 2008-09 it was 100 per cent.

**Table 1.4: Trends in Credit-Deposit Ratio (*India and Tamil Nadu*)**

| Sl. No. | Year | Credit - Deposit Ratio | |
|---|---|---|---|
| | | Tamil Nadu | India |
| 1. | 1974-75 | 96 | 69 |
| 2. | 1984-85 | 99 | 69 |
| 3. | 1989-90 | 103 | 66 |
| 4. | 1995-96 | 99 | 60 |
| 5. | 2004-05 | 90 | 57 |
| 6. | 2005-06 | 81 | 56 |
| 7. | 2006-07 | 86 | 57 |
| 8. | 2007-08 | 90 | 58 |
| 9. | 2008-09 | 100 | 67 |

*Source:* Tamil Nadu—An Economic Appraisal, Directorate of Evaluation and Applied Research, Chennai, 2008-2009.

## STATEMENT OF THE PROBLEM

The banking sector has been playing a crucial role in a developing economy. A dynamic and vibrant banking sector has emerged as a sector of the masses rather than that of the classes these days. The balanced distribution of the bank branches could ensure both quantitative and qualitative improvements in the economy, at large. In order to optimise the benefits of the banks and serve the requirements of multistructuralism, an egalitarian approach based on the 'Area matrix' has been well conceived and implemented throughout India from 1969 onwards. Consequently, the Lead Bank Scheme was born and started bearing creditable fruits, particularly, in rural-dominated segments of the economy. The Lead Bank leads all other agencies and organisations and co-ordinates their functions suitably well.

The central and state governments have introduced several subsidy schemes such as Prime Minister Rozgar Yojana (PMRY), Swarnajayanthi Gram Swarozgar Yojana (SGSY),

Swarna Jayanthi Shahari Rozgar Yojana (SJSRY) and Tamil Nadu Adi Dravida Housing Development Corporation (TAHDCO) for the upliftment of the weaker sections of the community. The loans, sanctioned under these programmes, come under priority sector lending. The bank credit for these programmes is included in the district credit plan.

The District Credit Plan is an essential part of the Lead Bank Scheme. The district credit plan covers particularly, the priority sector activities in rural areas. The credit plan provides a connecting link between the bank's lending for priority sector activities and the government's subsidy programmes for such activities. The Lead Bank implements the credit plans with the help of various financial agencies including commercial banks and monitors the overall performance. The Indian Overseas Bank is the Lead Bank in Kanyakumari District.

The impact of Government-sponsored scheme on beneficiaries before and after utilizing the bank credit, in terms of income, asset and employment generation will be examined and evaluated in this research exercise. The parameters, perspectives and problems pertaining to repayment and recovery of loans will also be highlighted.

The present study is carried out with the sprit of exploration of facts and hence it is expected to present original and creative types of knowledge in this area.

## OBJECTIVES OF THE STUDY

The specific objectives of the study are:

- To analyse and compare the trend and growth of advances made by commercial banks under Lead Bank Scheme to Government-sponsored schemes and priority sector;
- To find out the trend in demand, collection and recovery position of commercial banks;
- To measure and compare the amount of disbursement in terms of equity angles amongst the blocks;

- To evaluate the impact of Government sponsored schemes on the beneficiaries before and after availing the bank credit, in terms of income, asset and employment generation;
- To identify the factors influencing the repayment of loan by the borrowers;
- To analyse repayment and recovery performance and the views of the bankers and the beneficiaries;
- To offer suggestions on the basis of the findings of the study.

## PERIOD OF THE STUDY

This study was analysed on the basis of the primary data collected for one year from April 2008 to March 2009. The secondary data relating to the implementation of lead bank schemes and their respective performance available in the relevant documents for the year 1999-2000 to 2008-2009 were collected.

## METHODOLOGY

Designing suitable methodology and selection of analytical tools is important for a meaningful analysis of any research problem. This section is devoted to the statement of the methodology, which includes collection of data, sampling procedure and tools of analysis.

### Collection of Data

Both primary and secondary data have been used for the present study. A reconnaissance survey was made among the selected beneficiaries to get acquainted with the loan amount received, utilized and repaid. On the basis of the information gathered, a well-designed pre-tested interview schedule was drafted and used in the field survey to collect the primary data. Before undertaking the main survey, a tentative interview schedule was prepared and administered to 25 beneficiaries, in order to test the validity of the interview schedule. It facilitated the removal of the non-response and unwanted questions and the modified final schedule based on this were prepared.

The selected beneficiaries were contacted in person and the objectives of the study were clearly explained to them and their co-operation was ensured. The details regarding the general characteristics of the sample beneficiaries, their families, income, expenditure and savings, relating to the overall objectives of the study were collected from the sample beneficiaries, through the direct personal interview method.

Secondary data have been mainly collected from Annual Credit Plan of Lead bank in Kanyakumari district, RBI bulletins, periodicals, government publications, journals, newspapers, published and unpublished thesis.

## Sampling Procedure

The Lead bank beneficiaries are the sample population. The researcher has selected the stratified random sampling method. The following Table shows the sample distribution:

**Table 1.5: Distribution of Sample Respondents**

| Sl. No. | Sample | Target | No.of Respondents | Rejection | Sample |
|---|---|---|---|---|---|
| 1. | Non-agricultural sector | 300 (60) | 232 (77.33) | 34 (14.66) | 198 |
| 2. | Agricultural sector | 200 (40) | 156 (78) | 54 (34.62) | 102 |
| | **Total** | **500 (100)** | **388 (77.6)** | **88 (22.68)** | **300** |

The above Table shows that 500 samples were targeted, out of which 300 samples were from non-agricultural sector and 200 samples from agricultural sector. However, in non-agricultural sector 232 respondents responded (response rate 77.33%) out of which 34 samples were rejected (rejection rate on responded sample is 14.66%) thus 198 respondents were taken as find sample size for non-agricultural sector.

In the case of agricultural sector, out of the targeted 200 samples, 156 respondents responded (response rate 78%) and 54 respondents were rejected (rejection rate on responded sample is 34.62%). Thus 102 respondents were taken as final sample size from agricultural sector.

## Tools of Analysis

In order to analyse the average of branch's deposits, advances, lending, outstanding and recovery and its stability over the period, the arithmetic means (x) and co-efficient of variation (C.V) were calculated.

The trend and compound growth rates are computed by using semi log trend equation of the following form:

$$\text{Log } Y = a + bt \qquad \ldots (1.1)$$

Where

$Y$ = variable

$t$ = Time variable

and $a$ and $b$ are the parameters to be estimated.

The compound growth rate was calculated by using the following formula.

$$\text{Compound Growth Rate (\%)} = [\text{Antilog } b - 1] \times 100 \qquad \ldots (1.2)$$

The taxonomic method has been used to evaluate the Lead Bank Scheme in commercial banks in terms of growth and equity.

In order to identify the factors which influence the repayment, the following form of multiple log linear regression model was estimated:

$$\text{Log } Y = \beta_0 + \beta_1 \log X_1 + \beta_2 \log X_2 + \beta_3 \log X_3 + \beta_4 \log X_4 + U \qquad \ldots (1.3)$$

Where,

$Y$ = Annual repaid amount in rupees

$X_1$ = Loan amount received in rupees

$X_2$ = Annual net income received from the ventures in rupees

$X_3$ = Annual family income including other source in rupees

$X_4$ = Number of instalments

$U$ = Disturbance term

$\beta_0, \beta_1$ ....... 4 are the parameters to be estimated.

The above model was estimated by the method of least squares. The percentage recovery is calculated by using following formula

$$R = \frac{C}{D} \times 100 \qquad \text{... (1.4)}$$

Where

$R$ = Recovery percentage

$C$ = Collected amount and

$D$ = Demand

## LIMITATIONS OF THE STUDY

The present study is subjected to the following limitations:

1. The study is confined to the commercial banks under Lead Bank Scheme, lending to government-sponsored employment schemes;
2. The study pertains to the period of ten years from 1999-2000 to 2008-09;
3. The sample size of the study has been purposively determined for the study.

## CHAPTER SCHEME

This thesis entitled "A Study of Lead Bank Schemes in Kanyakumari District" is presented in seven chapters:

*Chapter I* introduces the subject and deals with Lead Bank Schemes, Service Area Approach, Government-sponsored employment schemes, Commercial banking in Tamil Nadu, Statement of the problem, Objectives, Period of study, Methodology, Tools of analysis, Limitations and Chapter scheme.

*Chapter II* discusses the review of literature related to bank advances, particularly, the lending pattern of the commercial banks to the Government - sponsored employment schemes.

*Chapter III* explains the functions and organizational structure of lead bank.

*Chapter IV* deals with the trend and growth of commercial bank advances, outstanding and recovery position.

*Chapter V* evaluates the Lead Bank Schemes, block-wise comparison of growth and equity angles.

*Chapter VI* analyses the impact of lead bank lending, in terms of income, asset and employment generation. Further, it examines the factors influencing the repayment of loan and recovery performance. Finally, it deals with the bankers' view and the views of the beneficiaries.

*Chapter VII* presents the summary of findings, suggestions and conclusion.

## REFERENCES


1. Reserve Bank of India, *Functions and Working*, 5th Edition 2001, p. 238.
2. *Ibid.*
3. *Ibid.*
4. *Ibid.*
5. *Ibid.*
6. *Annual Credit Plan — 2007-08*, Published by Lead Bank Section IOB, Nagercoil.
7. *Ibid.*
8. Reserve Bank of India, *Functions and Workings*, 5th Edition, p. 238.
9. Tara Chand, *Policies of Poverty Alleviation, General studies for UPSC Civil Servant, Preliminary Examination*, Tata McGraw Hills Winning Edge Series, 2003, pp. 23-28.
10. *Economic Survey*, 2005-06, Government of India.
11. Reena Verma, *Poverty and Poverty Alleviation Programmes*, Spectrum Hand Book of General Studies Spectrum Book of Publishers Ltd, 2003, p. 76.

12. Meenashi Anand Chandhary "Empowering Strategies for Rural Women in India" *Kurukshetra*, Vol. XLIV No. 6, 1996.
13. *Annual Credit Plan*, Published by the Lead Bank Section of IOB, Nagercoil.
14. *Ibid.*
15. *Ibid.*
16. *Ibid.*
17. *Economic Appraisal 2002-03*, Evaluation and Applied Research Department, Government of Tamil Nadu, Chennai.
18. *Ibid.*

2

# Review of Literature

## INTRODUCTION

This chapter presents a review of the existing literature, in order to gain insight into the research work undertaken in this area. Such review would facilitate the researcher to have a comprehensive knowledge of the concepts used in the earlier studies and enable better understanding of the facts of the subject under study.

## REVIEW OF LITERATURE

Hamumantha Rao,C.H.[1] highlighted the growth and expansion of institutional credit, particularly through commercial banking. The period after independence has been divided by him three phases. They are:

1. The early fifties to the late sixties, when the major policy objectives were in replacement of the informal sources;
2. The period from the late sixties to the early eighties, that witnessed the nationalisation of leading commercial banks and the massive expansion in the branches of commercial banks in rural areas; and

3. The last phase which starts in the early eighties, with the beginning of the Sixth Five Year Plan, characterized by growing overdues in respect of loan repayment, loan waivers and write-offs. Rao 'raises the policy issues, relating to the viability of credit institutions, equitable access to credit, and redefinition of priority sector and enhanced role of rural banking institutions, to cope up with the emerging challenges. It is necessary for the development role of institutional credit to complement by infrastructure and technology. In the credit plans, more emphasis should be on non-farm and allied agricultural activities.

Singh, C.P.[2] presented a brief review of various efforts to reduce poverty. The First Plan (1951-1956) accepted reduction in inequalities of income as one of its objectives. The Second Plan (1956-61) made added emphasis to it. The Third and Fourth Plans (1961-1966 to 1969-1974) highlighted the need for employment, and creation and distribution of income. They also identified scheduled castes and scheduled tribes as the major segments of the poor.

The most important programme of the Fifth Five Year Plan (1974-1979) was the 'Minimum Needs programme', while integrated Rural Development Programme (IRDP) was the central pillar of poverty eradication programme. During the Sixth Plan (1980-1985), Rural Landless Employment Guarantee Programme (RLEGP) was implemented to create more employment. In the Seventh Plan period (1985-1990) IRDP was made an effective instrument of poverty alleviation. Many gaps and weaknesses in the working of this programme kept the progress slow.

Prasad, H.[3] found that anti-poverty programme had direct impact on resource endowment employment and skill development. The success of this programme was limited. As pointed out by the Planning Commission, the constraints of these programmes were not coming from financial side but from organisational inadequacies and lack of clear-cut plan of development of the area towards which co-ordinated efforts of all concerned agencies should be directed.

Laxmi Narayanan, H.[4] studied three schemes of poverty alleviation programmes and found that TRYSEM had benefited nearly 3.32 lakhs schedule caste and schedule tribe youth, out of 9.4 lakhs who were trained. NREP was another centrally-sponsored scheme which funded on a 50:50 sharing basis between the centre and the states to generate additional employment opportunities in rural areas, to create community assets, to strengthen the rural infrastructure and to improve the nutritional standard of the rural poor. The wage was supposed to be paid in accordance with the wage rates notified under the Minimum Wage Act.

Pothulum,C. and Someshwar, K.[5] made a study on labour absorption through IRDP in the Mothobur block in Nalgonda district, to analyse the employment opportunities, generated under various schemes of IRDP and the nature of the job opportunities generated by the total of 327 economically active household numbers, 68 per cent of whom were, self-employed and rest of them wage earners. About 66 per cent of the cultivators were self-employed and 11 per cent of the family members were wage-employed. In the service sector of the rural artisan households, 90 per cent were self-employed. Among the agricultural labour households, half of the family members were self-employed and the rest engaged in wage employment.

The analysis of labour absorption through IRDP showed that various schemes and programmes had helped in the generation of employment opportunities to the rural poor. Employment generation was far below the benefits anticipated by the IRDP Manuals.

According to Iyer,K.[6] the primary objective of Jawahar Rozgar Yojana (JRY) was to generate employment through manaul labour and the secondary object was to create durable community assets, in the process of employment generation.

According to official statistics, 3,300 millions mandays were generated under JRY in the country, during the period from 1980-1990 to 1993-1994. The JRY was operated uniformly all over the country, without specifically focussing on the backward districts in the states. A policy shift occurred in the second half of 1993. Accordingly, two significant changes were made. The first was the change in criteria for allocation of funds to districts. Formerly, the district-wise allocation was made, using an index of backwardness formulated on certain criteria. But later, the central government changed this norm to include only two parameters, namely, proportion of rural SC/ST population to total SC/ST population in a district and the proportion of rural SC/ST population to total SC/ST population in a State. The main implications were:

1. District with low agricultural productivity, got higher JRY allocation;
2. Weightage for SC/ST population decreased from 60 per cent to 50 per cent; and
3. No more weightage was given for percentage of agricultural labourers.

Erappa,S.[7] found that the land held by SC/ST was 7.6 per cent of the land holdings in Karnataka (Chinappa Commission Report, 1990) and it was estimated that more than 70 per cent of the SC/ST beneficiaries utilized IRDP in Karnataka. The distribution of schemes, promoted under the broad heads of SC/ST showed that dairy occupied the first place, accounting for about 53 per cent of the total schemes, assisted by IRDP. It was found that SC/ST beneficiaries were gradually delinking their traditional occupation and getting into the main stream of production process. A little less than 50 per cent of the animal husbandry schemes were allowed to SC/ST beneficiaries. Thus IRDP programme helped more number of SC/ST beneficiaries to move above the poverty line.

Datt, R.[8] reviewed Jawahar Rozgar Yojana, and found that in the earlier employment programme, Central and State assistance was stipulated and found that central assistance would finance 80 per cent and the states share would be 20 per cent.

The main objectives were:

- Generation of gainful employment for the unemployed and underemployed men and women in rural areas;
- Creation of sustained employment by strengthening the rural infrastructure;
- Creating a community of social assets;
- Creating assets, in favour of the poor, for their direct and Continuing benefit;
- To bring about overall improvement in the quality of life in rural areas.

Wages under JRY were paid at the rate notified for the prescribed schedule of employment, under the Minimum Wage Act for relevant works.

Margaret Berger, N.[9] in her paper titled "Giving Women Credit: The Strength and Limitations of Credit as a Tool for Alleviating Poverty" examines the programmes and institutions, involved in lending to women micro-entrepreneurs, assesses the poverty alleviation potential of different credit models and reviews the effects of policy interventions in financial market in women's access to and use of credit. The programmes which aim to accomplish poverty alleviation, income and employment generation are bank schemes, intermediary programmes and parallel programmes of the banks. The last three channels have been found to be more effective than the first in improving womens' access to credit.

Sydney Ruth Schuler,C. Hashemi, S.M. and Riley, A.P.[10] in their study, have examined the impact of credit programmes and women's empowerment on contraceptive use, among rural women in Bangladesh. In this study, empowerment has been measured by mobility, ability to make small purchases, ability to make layer purchases, involvement in major decisions and relative freedom from domination within the family, political and legal awareness, participation in public protests and political campaigning and economic security and contribution to family support. The findings suggest that women's participation in credit programmes, in Bangladesh, increased the use of contraceptives. Only mobility, freedom from domination within the family, and economic security and contribution to family support had statistical effects in contraceptive use.

Khandker's, S.R.[11] study, from a 1991-1992 survey, is distinctive. Lay findings from Khandker's study highlight the significant impact of credit access provided by three largest micro finance institutions in Bangladesh: the Grameen Bank, Bangladesh Rural Advancement Committee (BRAC) and Rural Development Project-12 (RD-12). Among other findings, Khandker's study shows that credit access helps to lift about 5 per cent of participatory households, above the official poverty line each year. Khandker also highlights gender differences in programme impact. He discusses the impact on household consumption of the credit programmes to be approximately twice as long for female borrowers as for male borrowers.

Pallavi Chavan,T. and Ramkumar, R.[12] attempt to judge the performance of NGO-led micro-credit programmes and institutions-implemented, across various developing countries. The review indicated that NGO-led micro credit programmes and institutions such as Grameen Bank have been successful in reaching their target groups of poor, more effectively than the state-led programmes and institutions. The study also found that micro-credit programmes and institutions have generated a positive change in the incomes of beneficiaries though it is marginal. It also found that micro-credit programmes and institutions have generated a positive impact on the number of days of family employment even though their performance in the generation of wage employment has been poor.

Chowdhery,P.[13] discovered that the credit requirements of the farmers were of different types and for different purposes. For example, the seasonal credit needs were for meeting the various current input requirements such as purchase of seeds, fertilizers and pesticides, medium term credit requirements were for the purchase of seeds, drills and sprayers and long term credit needs were for purposes such as levelling of land, for the construction of cattle sheds etc.

Joshi, P.L.[14] concluded that a single financial institution, with family substantial resources meeting different needs of the agriculturists, has its attraction instead of presently-accepted multi-agency approach. The results reveal that loans borrowed from the State Bank of India, by the active farmers for crop production purposes were not very helpful in increasing the productivity of land vis-a-vis non participation farmers.

Jha, N.[15] traces the origin of Land Development Banks and Co-operatives at the world level. Germany is the original home of land banks and co-operatives. The co-operatives are known as Landschaftan in this country. The first bank of landschaft was created in 1769. Jha then discusses the emergence of Land Development Banks in India, particularly in Bihar.

Dandekar, V.M.[16] has traced the development of agricultural credit in India during the 19th and 20th centuries. The development of co-operative finance and supply of agricultural credit by commercial banks and Regional Rural Banks (RRB) is evaluated. The finances at the time of Independence were available to agriculturists from the government departments, co-operatives and to a small extent, from the commercial banks. The most important source was money lenders. Several committees later have mentioned about the poor health of agricultural credit institutions. These committees ended up recommending bypasses to let the credit flow around the overdues. Overdues are mounting in agricultural credit. The new thinking about agricultural credit is contained in the reports of the Credit Review Committee (1989) and the Committee on Financial System (Narasimman Committee Report, 1991). But both the committees fail to consider how to reorganise the structure of rural credit. Many committees noted the weak base (the primary credit societies) of the entire co-operative credit structure. But these committees did not realize that the primary societies are weak because their lending business is essentially non-viable. To reorganise the present banking system, commercial as well as co-operatives, it is suggested that:

1. Various co-operative credit institutions should be allowed to function so long as they are commercially viable. Otherwise, they should be gradually phased out.
2. The commercial banks should be reorganised according to the suggestions given by the Committee on Financial System (1991).
3. The reorganisation of the banking structure should consist of:
   *(a)* three or four large banks (including the State Bank of India) which could become international in character;
   *(b)* ten national banks with a network of branches throughout the country;
   *(c)* local banks whose operations could be generally confined to specific regions; and
   *(d)* rural banks (including RRBs) whose operation would be confined to the rural areas, mainly to finance agriculture and allied activities. Owing to the present day complexities, no single bank can serve all the sectors. Hence, each bank, at least the nationalised banks, should be asked to progressively specialise in one or more areas and withdraw from the rest.

Singh, R.K.P. and Upadhayaya, K.M.[17] studied the recoveries in the Regional Rural Banks, operating in Bihar and reported that loan recoveries in RRBs declined continuously during the period 1978-1980. The reasons for the decline or low loan recoveries were: inadequate arrangement for recovery in bank branches and shortage of funds with the borrowers to repay the loan either due to crop failure or expenditure on festivals and ceremonies or other social functions or illness of family members. Inadequate follow up by banks for repayment and wilful default were also important reasons for declining loan recoveries in RRBS.

Sahar, B.[18] in his study on the repayment of Dairy Loans, financed under IRDP in Goraul Block in the district of Muzaffarpur, found that dairy being profitable enterprise, should be encouraged, in order to enable diversification of the farm business by providing proper and adequate supply of production credit so that, the beneficiaries may adopt this business on scientific and commercial lines. Before lending, the lending institutions may use the prediction criteria on the basis of significant factors which may enable them to know the category to which the prospective borrowers belonged and this would reduce the risk they face in lending to the borrowers.

Rajagopalan, V.[19] had defined agricultural credit, as the amount of investment funds that could be made available for farm production, from sources outside that of the farm. He had also defined agricultural credit as the amount of investment funds that could be made available for the purpose of development and sustenance of farm production and productivity.

Yadava *et al.*,[20] found that adopting improved agricultural technology required greater amounts of money by way of investment. It was more so in the case of small farmers who were frequently confronted with the problem of resources. The study showed that all the small farmers who came under study required credit.

Pranab Bardhan, L. and Ashok Rudra,K.[21] have examined the terms and conditions of land, labour and credit relations. They observed, that apart from professional money-lenders, there were rich farmers who practised money-lending and were not confined to backward villages alone. While conducting surveys in West Bengal, Bihar and Eastern U.P., they noted that there were even cases of landlords, giving consumption loans free of interest, and also of advances made by them to meet the production needs of borrowers, free of interest. An interesting point to note is that though loans were given free of interest, there existed also the practice of rendering of small services to the landlord by the tenant borrowers. Sometimes, the tenants' dependence on the landlord was associated with or reinforced by dependence of other members of the tenants' household. The tenant and the other members worked for the same landlord, under exploitative conditions. Throughout the study area, the practice of 'bonded labour', labour tied to a particular creditor for an indefinite period until loans taken in the past were repaid, prevailed. West Bengal, Bihar and Eastern U.P. reported cases of bonded labour.

The overwhelming need to make an assessment of the overall credit situation in the rural sector was first sought to be properly addressed during the 1930's. The Banking Enquiry Committee (1930)[22] sought to arrive at a starting figure for the overall short and intermediate term-credit, required by the cultivators in British India. According to the Committee, the lower limit lay somewhere between Rs. 300 crores and Rs. 400 crores. It was, however, only after independence that concerted efforts, to evaluate the rural credit situation, got off the ground. The pursuance of its professed policies, the Government of India gave primary importance to the agricultural and rural sector in its development agenda. It was realized that rural indebtedness constituted the most daunting and formidable barrier to revitalise the rural economy.

The RBI Survey (1971-72) analysed the outstanding liabilities of the rural households, according to the purpose for which liabilities had been incurred. Out of the total cash debt of Rs. 3,752 crores outstanding against all rural households, Rs. 1,876 crores, representing nearly one-half, was incurred for production purposes, and the rest for 'other purposes'. Debts of less than Rs. 500 formed only 9 per cent of the total, while those between Rs. 500 and 1000 constituted 11 per cent. Debts exceeding Rs. 1000 accounted for 80 per cent of the total debts and the debt group between Rs. 2000 and Rs. 5000 formed the largest chunk in the total.

The Rural Labour Enquiry Committee,[23] (1974-75), in its final report, analysed the incidence and extent of indebtedness among rural households. The report pointed out that in most of the states, majority of the households were in debt. A comparison between households with cultivated land and without cultivated land showed that the incidence of indebtedness was higher in all states among households with land, than those without land. At the all-India level, the incidence of indebtedness was 71 per cent among households with cultivated land and about 48 per cent among households without cultivated land.

A notable feature observed by the All-India Survey 1981, was that the proportion of indebted households had decreased quite sharply from 43 per cent in 1971 to 20 per cent in 1981. The average debt per household, on the other hand, increased from Rs. 503 to Rs. 661. The available literature on rural credit, suggests that a large proportion of the growing credit requirements, arises from the capital needs of the cultivator households particularly, those with medium and large size in terms of fixed assets. The highest percentage-wise increase is observed in the demand for medium size, medium term loans for production purposes among the medium asset group. This section of cultivators had also been the biggest beneficiaries of the supply of institutional credit.

Mahendra D. Desai and Bharat D. Naik,[24] while analysing the demand for short-term credit, found in 1971, that at the time when the high-yielding variety programme was being introduced, the demand for credit remained largely unmet mainly, because of the non-availability of credit to small farmers. The institutions then used to select farmers for granting credit in general, from bigger cultivators. Inspite of the avowed policy objective of a multi-agency approach for meeting credit requirements of the cultivators, it was the large farmers, who in fact constituted the biggest beneficiaries. The evidence was that commercial banks provided Rs. 210.40 crores, by way of short-term and medium-term credit to agriculture of which the bulk went, however, to the above-average farmers.

Sharma, J.S. and Prasad, B.[25] in a study conducted in three selected districts of Uttar Pradesh analysed the change in demand for credit due to changes in the technology of agricultural production. They pointed out, that at the then existing level of technology, the credit needs of the sample households were of the tune of Rs. 114 lakhs, of which about 35 per cent, 29 per cent and 36 per cent were needed by small, medium and large farmers respectively. With improved technology, the credit needs would be Rs. 367 lakhs, of which 30 per cent, 20 per cent and 50 per cent would be required by small, medium and large farmers respectively. One striking feature of the growth in credit observed was that the credit requirements of larger farmers increased more rapidly than those of small and medium farmers. Use of credit increased the income even at the prevailing levels of technology. More adoption of improved technology, unassociated with the increase in credit use was not found to increase the income of farmers to any significant extent.

Meanwhile, the credit requirements of the low asset group, namely landless labourers, artisans, petty traders, etc., were also on the increase but the institutional credit failed to make significant contributions to this requirement. As a result, this class, which is historically most susceptible to chronic indebtedness, depended for most part of its credit needs, on non-institutional agencies, which charged arbitrary rates of interest.

We shall now take up studies which have examined the question of determinants of loan requirements and the extent of default among the various sections of borrowers. The role of the organized sector in the money market, and the variations of interest rates prevailing therein also will be examined in this context.

Devaprakash, R.[26] noted that the quantum of credit requirement for agricultural purposes which was only Rs. 1,130 crores in 1969, grew twenty-fold by 1989. Despite the manifold increase in availability, only over 23 per cent of the total number of operational holdings received credit. Devaprakash has emphasized the need for concerted efforts to invigorate the credit market and for fine tuning of the credit discipline.

Arun Kumar Bandopadhya, R.[27] notes that in traditional agriculture, where the distribution of resources is unequal, a section of the farm community takes loans, mainly, for consumption purposes, from another section, at high rates of interest. The high rates of interest in such societies are mainly due to high risk premium and administration costs involved, and only partly due to monopolistic and monopsonistic elements in the credit market. The prevalence of high rates of interest, in these underdeveloped areas, is also due to the fact that a substantial part of the borrowing is used for consumption purposes and therefore the demand for such loans is highly inelastic. An interesting finding of this study is that the loans contracts which do not explicitly make mention of rates of interest charged, do, in fact, carry very high implicit rates.

Mohan Rao, J.[28] in his article on interest rates in backward agriculture, explains the determination of interest rates on the basis of collateral valuation. The lender's gain consists of two components viz., monopoly power and default. Monopoly power in the credit market enables the lender to value collateral below their normal price. In such a situation, default means loss to the borrower, as the lender can raise interest rates substantially.

Atiqur Rahman,T.[29] examined credit relations in two survey areas in Bangladesh. The monetary and in-kind rates of interest, charged by money-lenders were about 100 and 150 per cent per annum. Marketing intermediaries also charged interest at similar high rates. Rates of interest charged by landlords hovered between 50 and 100 per cent per annum. Thus, in general:

1. the rates of interest on loans from non-institutional sources were very high;
2. rates of interest charged by landlords were not as high as those by professional money-lenders and marketing intermediaries; and
3. in-kind rates were higher than monetary rates of interest.

Anthony Bottemley,L.[30] suggests that strict repayment discipline must be established early in any rural credit programme, if default is to be kept within manageable limits. But the problem was that Government often has neither the resources nor the political will to enforce repayments.

Acharya *et al.*,[31] pointed out that the smallest farmers utilized as high as 95 per cent of loans for consumption while the percentage for large farmers was only 23.4. The small and medium size farmers who were hard-hit, financially were forced to use relatively substantial proportions of loans for direct consumption.

Vashisht,S.K.[32] found out in his study on a particular area which was agriculturally advanced, that 88 per cent of the loans were utilized for production purposes, while the remaining 12 per cent was utilized for consumption. The utilization pattern indicated that among production purposes, fertilizer loans which accounted for 64 per cent of the total credit was the most dominant. Social and religious ceremonies which accounted for 5 per cent of the total credit, topped the list among non-productive purposes.

According to Nicholson, R.[33] the main purpose for which an agriculturist needed money was to pay for current cultivation expenses and for family expenses. The agricultural credit was not only essential but also inevitable for the farmers and as such, it should be considered neither as objectionable nor as a sign of weakness.

Meclichar Emmanual,K.[34] had argued that credit involved a temporary transfer of wealth and included the amounts, provided by way of loans or advances, cash credit of advances, overdrafts or purchase of discount bills other than advances against security, or by way of purchase of demand documentary bills, drawn in connection with the movement of a commodity.

Johl, S.S. and Singh.B.P.[35] found that in Punjab, the Government and the co-operative institutions were not meeting the full requirements of the development finance, required by the farmers.

Bhargava,V.K. and Shah,S.L.[36] pointed out that the credit needs of the farmers consisted of the purchase of credit for fertilizers, for hired labour, for pumpset, for land reclamation, for machinery and for agricultural equipments. The adoption of new technology was capital-intensive in nature, which would lead to a manifold increase in the credit demanded.

Dra Srivastava *et al.*,[37] had recommended that as far as possible, credit should be advanced in kind, and the small and the medium farmers should be brought under the scheme of supervised credit.

Ghosal, S.N.[38] is of the view that:

1. the conditions that exist in Indian agriculture would provide the stimuli of capital and leadership to this sector; and
2. the Indian farmers should be provided with alternative leadership and institutional leadership may be encouraged.

It is recommended that loans should be provided not only on the basis of value of land but also on the basis of value of crop to be raised on that land. The co-operative structure may be adopted for serving and supervising the loans to the farmers.

Subramaniyan, K.V. and Patel, R.K.[39] in their study on farmers' income in Andhra Pradesh concluded that credit had helped all groups of farmers to increase their net farm income in the various zones.

According to Kopkin et.al.,[40] agricultural finance referred to the acquiring and controlling of assets, ownership by way of cash purchase, borrowings, leasing in and custom hiring.

Agarwal, M.L. and Kumawat, R.K.[41] had proved that the provision of additional credit had increased farm incomes, even at the then existing levels of technology, by 41 per cent, whereas adoption of new technology, without additional credit, had not resulted in any increase in the yield and adoption of improved technology, with additional capital in the form of credit, had increased the farm income enormously. Similar arguments had been advanced by Singh,[42] Subramanian[43] and Pandy.[44]

Shukla, B.D. and Mishra, S.D,[45] in their study Co-operative on credit in Uttar Pradesh had concluded that there was a positive impact of the co-operative finance on the levels of input, income and employment.

According to Sain, K.[46] co-operative credit can also result in the upliftment of agriculture by encouraging the farmers to increase their own irrigation potential, to enable them to use chemical fertilizers, high yielding varieties of seeds, pesticides and adopt modern techniques so that they can adopt the multiple cropping patterns.

Ramadass, M.[47] had studied the demand for and the productivity of the provision of farm credit in the Pondicherry region. This study had found that farm credit had a positive and significant impact on the productivity of small and medium farms.

Srivastava, K.[48] had attempted to study the impact of farm credit with different levels of parameters. The study had disclosed a high positive marginal productivity of capital among all the groups of farmers who had utilized a less than optimum level of credit. The production of crops and the net profits had increased with every successive additional unit of credit.

There are many studies, in which the importance of institutional credit in agriculture, in the context of new technology and agricultural development, has been discussed. Dasgupta,T.[49] concentrates mainly on technological changes in relation to productivity by taking into account the changing class relations in the historic context. She arrives at the conclusions that technological changes will make a positive contribution but would depend upon the horizontal and vertical spread of technology. She further observes that there is little contribution of the new technology to improve the overall living conditions, and the quality of life in the rural areas. In future, the effect of new technology on these aspects will depend on:

1. the public policies, to regulate labour and land market;
2. the control of choice of factor combinations on larger farms; and
3. the investing part of the surplus, originating in agriculture.

Singh *et al.*,[50] made an attempt to study the impact of credit on farmers by comparing the beneficiaries and non-beneficiaries with the help of a few indicators such as the cropping pattern and the cropping intensity and they had indicated that there was a more significant development in the case of the beneficiaries as compared to the non-beneficiaries.

Chitranjan,D.[51] was of the view that creditworthiness could also be improved by increasing the application of production techniques, which resulted in saving land and using more of labour as the small and the marginal farmers had abundance of labour and scarcity of land resources.

Creditworthiness could also be improved by evolving a production pattern which was market oriented and biased against self-consumption. An obvious implication of such an approach would be to encourage the small farmers and the marginal farmers to switch over to the cultivation of more and more of the cash crops.

The institutional credit requirements are estimated by Desai, D.K.[52] for the years 1990, 1995 and 2000 A.D. The total short-term credit requirements for the agricultural production sub-system, at the reduced level as per Alternative III were estimated at Rs. 14,050 crores in 1990, Rs. 2,89,700 crores in 1995 and Rs. 49,200 crores in 2000 A.D.

Kulwant Singh,N.[53] in his work entitled "Co-operative Agricultural Credit Utilisation in Himachal Pradesh" had analysed and concluded that in recent years, the requirements of agricultural credit had assumed significant dimensions due to the increasing thrust in the development of new technology in the agricultural sector.

Sankarama, R.[54] looked into some important aspects of co-operation in the economic field. The broad classification of themes covers "Bases of Co-operatives", 'Strategies for the Models of Tomorrow' and 'Co-operatives in the Emerging Context'. The main conclusion of Sankarama's study is that the problem of rural leadership is different from that of other leaderships. This leadership plays a significant role in shaping the social, cultural, political and economic life of rural population. The leadership qualities in rural areas can be seen to be power-oriented, achievement oriented and affiliation-oriented.

Mitra,S. and Lahiri,D.[55] have evaluated the expectations from the co-operatives. A potential borrower will have to depend on the money-lender with whom he has more personal relation. This dependence on a single money-lender confers a monopoly of power on the money-lender. This also results in an exorbitantly high rate of interest. It is suggested by many quarters that in order to reduce the poor producers' dependence on money lenders, consumption loans through co-operatives should be granted.

Mahalingam,N.[56] in his study stated that the bank credit is a key driver of development programmes. The entrepreneur is pivotal to add value to the economy and is in need of bank credit to facilitate investment so that products and services reach the consumers. Much stress is given to agriculture sector-lending in India, as 65 per cent of the population is engaged in agriculture. India has a set-goal to emerge as:

*(a)* a developed nation by 2020; and

*(b)* the third largest economy in the world by 2050.

Research investigations have revealed that the area under irrigation in the country can be expanded to 114.50 million hectares, with the adoption of micro irrigation against the 57.25 million hectares at present. Sustainable employment can be generated for all the economically active population. The above strategy for development of infrastructure can be implemented with an investment of (Rs.60, 000 × 11.45 crores) Rs.6, 87,000 crores within a span of 20-30 years.

Bank credit in India has to be expanded at least to 120 to 150 per cent of GDP to provide an accelerated push to the development of the economy of India and India can emerge as strong as the developed countries and become the third largest economy of the world by 2050.

Kulshrestha, U.C. in his article,[57] "Working and progress of Lead Banks - Restropect and Prospects", has analysed the problems in implementing the Lead Bank scheme. The study has emphasized the need for special powers to Lead banks to control the other banks in the district and to ensure effective monitoring and review the branch-wise progress in the district.

Amarjit Kahlon, R.,[58] in his article "Development - oriented service area approach of bank Branch's", has highlighted the concept of service area approach and the problems in formulating the village credit plans.

Subha Rao, B.[59] in his research study, entitled, "Study of commercial Bank Finance to Agriculture in Prakasam District - Andhra Pradesh", has analysed the areas such as pattern of utilisation of commercial bank credit, adequacy of scale of finance, credit needs of the farmers and the like. He also analysed the policies and procedures adopted by the commercial banks in financing agriculture.

Gokhale, H.V.,[60] in his research study, "A study of Bank of India as Lead Bank in Chandrapur District with special Emphasis on Priority Sector", has analysed the implementation of the Lead Bank Scheme in Chandrapur District of Maharastra State. The study mainly covers the bank-wise and sector-wise performance of targets set for the credit plans. The study has also analysed the impact of banks lending under Lead Bank Scheme on income and asset generation of beneficiaries.

## REFERENCES

1. Hamumantha Rao, C.H. "Policy Issues, Relating to Irrigation and Rural Credit in G.S. Bhallq (ed)", *Economic Liberalisation and Indian Agriculture,* Institution for Studies in Industrial Development, 1994, pp. 287-307.
2. Singh, C.P. "*Poverty Alleviation Programmes Under the Plans*", Indian Publishing Company, New Delhi, 1980, pp. 55-59.
3. Prasad, H. "Employment and Income in Rural India", *Economic and Political Weekly,* Vol. 7, No. 2, 1986, pp. 886-887.
4. Laxmi Narayanan, H. "Poverty Alleviation — Where has IRDP Gone Wrong?" *Economic Times,* 1986, pp. 17-21.
5. Pothulum C. and Someshwar, K. "Labour Absorption Through IRDP", *Rural India,* October-November, 1992, pp. 245-247.
6. Parameswaran Iyer, K. "Creating Rural Employment — JRYS New Thrust Area", *Economic and Political Weekly,* Vol. 21, No. 32, 1994, pp. 2065-2066.
7. Erappa, S. "IRDP Experience of SC/ST in Karnataka", *Southern Economist,* Vol. 33, No. 20, 1995, pp. 13-16.
8. Ruddar Datt, R. "Jawahar Rozgar Yojana — A Review", *Southern Economists,* Vol. 34, No. 10, 1995, pp. 5-8.
9. Margaret Berger,N. "Giving Women Credit: The Strengths and Limitations of Credit as a Tool for Alleviating Poverty", *World Development,* Vol. 17, No. 7. 1989, pp. 38-61.

10 Sydney Ruth Schuler, C. Hashemi, S.M. and Riley, A.P. "The Influence of Women's Changing Roles and Status in Bangladesh Fertility Transition: Evidence from a Study of Credit Programmes in Contraceptive Use", *World Development*, Vol. 25, No. 4, 1997, pp. 13-15.

11. Shahidur S.R. Khandker, *"Fighting Poverty with Micro Credit: Experience in Bangladesh"*, Oxford University Press, New York, 1988.

12. Pallavi Chavan, T. and Ramkumar,R. "Micro Credit and Rural Poverty: An analysis of Empirical Evidence", *Economic and Political Weekly*, Vol. XXXVII, No. 10, 2002.

13 Chowdhery, P. "Farm Credit Needs and the Role of Commercial Banks to Financing". *Indian Journal of Agricultural Economics*, Vol. 23, No. 3, 1968, pp. 22-28.

14. Joshi, P.L. "Institutional Financing in India", Deep and Deep Publication, New Delhi, 1985, p. 35.

15. Nand Kishore Jha, N. *"Bank Finance and Green Revolution in India,"* Amar Prakashan Publication, New Delhi, 1985, p. 36.

16. Dandekar, V.M. *"The Indian Economy 1947-1992, Agriculture"*, Sage Publication, Vol. I, New Delhi, 1994, pp. 212-236.

17. Singh, R.K.P. and Upadhayaya, K.M. "A Study of Loan Recovery of Regional Rural Bank in Bihar", *Finance Agriculture*, Vol. 16, No. 2, 1998, pp. 37-39.

18. Balram Sahar,B. *"A Study on Repayment of Dairy Loans Financed Under IRDP (Goraul, Block, Muzaffarpur District,)"*, Unpublished Thesis, Department of Agricultural Economics, RAO, Bihar, 2000.

19. Rajagopalan,V. "Farm Liquidity and Institutional Financing for Agricultural Development", *Indian Journal of Agriculture Economics*, Vol. 23, No. 4, 1968, pp. 25-30.

20. Yadava, J.P. Ramachandra, and Pandey, S.P. "Small Farmers and Their Credit Requirement: Its Availability and Sources"; *Indian Co-operative Review*, Vol. 7, No. 3, 1975, pp. 241-247.

21. Pranab Bardhan,L. and Ashok Rudra,K. "Interlinkages of Land, Labour and Credit Relations: An Analysis of Village Survey Data in East India", *Economic and Political Weekly*, Vol. 13, February 1993.

22. Reserve Bank of India, *All India Debt and Investment Survey*, 1971-72.

23. Rural Labour Enquiry Committee 1974-75, *Final Report on Indebtedness Among Rural Labour Households*, December 18, 1978.

24. Mahendra D. Desai and Bharat D. Naik, "Prospects of Demand for Short-Term Institutional Credit for High Yielding Varieties" *Indian*

*Journal of Agricultural Economics*, Vol. 26, No. 4, October-December, 1971, pp. 23-26.

25. Sharma, J.S. and Prasad, B. "An Assessment of Production Credit Needs in Developing Agriculture", *Indian Journal of Agricultural Economics*, Vol. 26, No. 4, October-December, 1971, pp. 26-29.
26. Devaprakash, R. "Agricultural Credit Need, Streamlining", *The Hindu*, Vol. 12, No. 157, July 4, 1989.
27. Arun Kumar Bandopadhya,R. "*Economics of Agricultural Credit with Special Reference to Small Farmers in West Bengal*", Institute of Economic Growth, New Delhi, 2000, p. 77.
28. Mohan Rao, J. "Interest Rates in Backward Agriculture", *Cambridge Journal of Economics*, Vol. 4, 1980, pp. 159-167.
29. Atiqur Rahman,T. "Usury Capital and Credit Relations in Bangladesh Agriculture: Some Implications for Capital Formation and Capitalist Growth", *Bangladesh Development Studies*, Vol. 7, No. 2, 1997.
30. Anthony Bottemley,L. "Interest Rate Determining in Underdeveloped Rural Areas", *American Journal of Agricultural Economics*, Vol. 57, No. 2, May 1975, pp. 35-39.
31. Acharya, T.K.T. Dhogade, M.C. and Lopes, M.M. "A Study of Credit Problems of Farmers in a Tribal Area of Maharashtra", *Agriculture and Agro-Industries Journal*, February, 1992, pp. 11-15.
32. Vashisht, S.K. "Distribution and Utilisation of Short-term Co-operative Credit on Hoshiapur District of Punjab", *Indian Co-operative Review*, Vol. XVIII, No. 3, April 1981, pp. 9-14.
33. Nicholson,R. "Report Regarding the Possibility of Introducing Agricultural Banks in Madras State", *Reserve Bank of India*, Vol. 1, No. 1, 1960, p. 3.
34. Meclichar Emmanual, K. "Farm Credit: On Credit Projections", *Indian Journal of Agricultural Economics*, Vol. 24, No. 4, 1984, pp. 117-137.
35. Johl, S.S. and Singh, B.P. "An Evaluation of Agricultural and Co-operative Credit in Punjab", *Indian Co-operative Review*, 1995, p. 850.
36. Bhargava, V.K. and Shah, S.L. "A Study of Credit Requirements and Advances to Farmers in Patiala District", *Indian Journal of Agricultural Economics*, Vol. 23, No. 3, 1986, pp. 38-42.
37. Dra Srivastava, D.H., Sirohi, A.S., Singh, D., and Singh, K.N. "Analysis of Productive Use of Credit in I.R.D.P. Shabad, Bombay", *Financing Agriculture*, Vol. 2, No. 2, 1980, pp. 1-4.

38. Ghosal, S.N. *Agricultural Financing in India*, Asia Publishing House, Bombay, 1992, pp. 287-308.

39. Subramaniyan, K.V. and Patel, R.K. "Impact of Capital Availability on Farm Income and Demand for Short Term Credit in West Godavari District, Andhra Pradesh", *Agricultural Situation in India*, Vol. 28, No. 3, 1983, pp. 149-152.

40. Hopkin, J.A., Barry P.G. and Baker, C.B. *"Financial Management in Agriculture"*, The Interstate Printer and Publisher Inc., New York, 1993, p. 3.

41. Agarwal, M.L. and Kumawat, R.K. "Potentialities of Increasing Farm Income through Credit and New Technology", *Agricultural Situation in India*, Vol. 28, No. 9, 1984, pp. 489-493.

42. Karan Singh and Ashwanikumar Garg, "Impact of Small Farmers Development Agencies on Their Beneficiaries in Punjab", *Financing Agriculture*, Vol. 7, No. 3, 1985, pp. 27-30.

43. Subramanian, R. "Impact Bank Credit and Technology on Net Return of Farmers in Coimbatore, Tamil Nadu", *Mysore Journal of Agricultural Science*, Vol. 10, No. 3, 1996, pp. 423-430.

44. Pandy, H.K. "Credit Need in Changing Agriculture", *Financing Agriculture*, Vol. 4, No. 1, 1983, pp. 18-21.

45. Shukla, B.D. and Mishra, S.D. "Impact of Co-operative Finance — A Case Study in a Block of Uttar Pradesh", *Financing Agriculture*, Vol. 6, No. 2, 1996, pp. 26-30.

46. Sain, K. "Role of Co-operative in Green Revolution — A Movement for Contemplation", *Indian Co-operative Review*, Vol. 11, No. 2, January 1994, pp. 61-65.

47. Ramadass, M. "Demand for and Productivity of Farm Credit in Pondicherry Region" *Economic Appraisal*, 1998, pp. 112-116.

48. Srivastava, K. "Estimation of Credit for Agriculture", *Financing Agriculture*, Vol. 4, No. 1, 1996, pp. 18-21.

49. Sipra Dasgupta,T. *"Class Relations and Technical Changes in Indian Agriculture"*, Institute of Economic Growth, New Delhi, 1980, p. 29.

50. Singh, G.N., Azad Rajeeva Srivastava, M.P. and Gupta, B.R. "Role of Land Development Bank in Raising Production, Productivity and Income in Agriculture", *Indian Co-operative Review*, Vol. 17, No. 3, 1980, pp. 58-60.

51. Chitranjan, D. "Credit Rationing—A Perspective", *Financing Agriculture*, Vol. 18, No. 324, July-December, 1986, pp. 8-10.

52. Desai, D.K. "Institutional Credit Requirements for Agricultural Production in 2000 A.D.", *Indian Journal of Agricultural Economics*, Vol. XLIII, No.3, July-December, 1988, pp. 326-355.
53. Kulwant Singh, N. "Co-operative Agricultural Credit Utilisation in Himachal Pradesh", *Finance India*, Vol. 10, No. 3, September, 1996, pp. 671-676.
54. Sankarama,R. "Pattern of Values of Rural Co-operative Leaders in India", *Institute of Rural Management*, 1996, pp. 38-61.
55. Mitra, S. and Lahiri, D. "Expectations from Co-operatives Belied or Misplaced, *Indian Co-operative Review*, Vol. 1, 1996, pp. 129-138.
56. Mahalingam, N. "Bank Credit for Economic Development", *Kisan World*, Vol. 32, No. 7, July, 2005, pp. 5-7.
57. Kulshrestha, U.C. "Working and Progress of Lead Banks - Restropect and Prospects", *Journal of Indian Institute of Bankers*, October-December, Vol. 56, No. 4, 1985, p. 232.
58. Amarjit Kahlon,R. "Development Oriented Service Area Approach of Bank Branch's", *National Bank News Review*, June-August, 1990, pp. 45-47.
59. Subha Rao, B. "Study of Commercial Bank Finance to Agriculture in Prakasam District — Andhra Pradesh", Unpublished Thesis, Banaras Hindu University, 1990.
60. Gokhale, H.V., "A Study of Bank of India as Lead Bank in Chandrapur District With Special Emphasis on Priority Sector", Unpublished Thesis, Nagpur University, Nagpur, 1990.

# 3

# Functions and Organisational Structure of Lead Bank

## INTRODUCTION

The Banking industry in India has made considerable progress, especially, during the last 3 decades, to emerge as one of the accredited agencies of rural development. The orientation towards rural economy gained momentum only after nationalization of major commercial banks. For various reasons, they took roots mainly in the urban and metropolitan centers and bulk of loans and advances was directed to large and medium scale industries. No serious attempt was made by banks to finance the agricultural sector.

The Co-operative Banking structure was assigned the main task of meeting credit requirement in the rural areas. Yet, the credit gap remained unfilled, even after supplementing the efforts of co-operatives. In fact, it started widening further, especially, after the Green Revolution in mid 60's, in view of the larger and increasing credit needs of Indian Agriculture. The above process necessitated commercial banks to join the force. This envisaged increasing lending to sectors like Agriculture, SSI and Services with emphasis, on borrowers of small means.

The National Credit Council was set up in December 1967 to determine the priorities of bank credit among various sectors of the economy. The NCC appointed a study group on the organizational framework for the implementation of social objectives in October 1968, under the Chairmanship of Prof. Dr. Gadgil. The study group found that the commercial banks had penetrated only 5000 villages as of June 1967 and out of the institutional credit to agriculture at 39 per cent, the share was negligible at one per cent, the balance being met by the co-operatives. The banking needs of the rural areas, in general, and backward areas in particular, were not taken care of by the commercial banks. Besides, the credit needs of agriculture, SSI and allied activities remained neglected. Therefore, the group recommended the adoption of an area-approach for bridging the spatial and structural credit gaps. Later, All India Rural Credit Review Committee, 1969, endorsed the view that commercial banks should increasingly come forward to finance activities in rural areas.

## GENESIS OF THE LEAD BANK SCHEME

The study group, which was presided over by Prof. Dr. Gadgil, recommended in October 1969, the adoption of an 'Area approach' for the development of credit and banking in the country, on the basis of local conditions. The group suggested earmarking of the districts to commercial banks, so that they could act as space-setters in the districts allotted, in providing integrated banking facilities. The Committee of Bankers, appointed by RBI, under the Chairmanship of Sr. F.K.F. Nariman, also endorsed this area approach. RBI accepted the recommendation and formulated the Lead Bank Scheme (LBS) in December 1969. Under the Scheme, each district had been assigned to different banks (public and private) to act as a consortium leader, to coordinate the efforts of banks in the district, particularly, in matters like branch expansion and credit planning. The LBS did not envisage a monopoly of banking business to Lead Bank in the district. The Lead Bank was to act as a consortium leader for co-ordinating the efforts of all credit institutions, in each of the allotted districts for expansion of branch banking facilities and for meeting the credit needs of the rural economy. In the meanwhile, nationalization of 14 major commercial banks in July 1969 (and another 6 banks in 1980), paved the way for bringing about dramatic changes in their operations. One of the important changes ushered in immediately, was the expansion of the branch network in the unbanked areas, with a view to bridge spatial gaps. Banks were directed to open a large number of branches in unbanked rural and semi-urban areas.

## Allotment of Districts Among the Lead Banks

All the districts in the country, excepting the metropolitan cities of Mumbai, Kolkata, Chennai and Union Territories of Chandigarh, Delhi and Goa, were allotted to public sector banks and a few private sector banks. Later on, the Union Territories of Goa, Daman and Diu as also the rural areas of the Union Territories of Delhi and Chandigarh have been brought within the purview of LBS.

## Impressionistic Surveys and Branch Expansion

The Lead Banks conducted impressionistic surveys during 1969-70 in their districts, to identify the potential for branch expansion and invoke the co-operation of other banks operating in the district, for branch expansion and financing the various union industries. This has resulted in massive branch expansion in the unbanked and underbanked areas.

## Formation of District Consultative Committees (DCCs)

The next important development in the history of LBS was the constitution of DCCs in all the districts, in the early seventies, to facilitate co-ordination of activities of all the banks and the financial institutions on the one hand and Government departments on the other. The DCCs were constituted in the lead districts during 1971-73.

## Study Groups on Lead Bank Scheme in Gujarat and Maharashtra

RBI constituted two study groups to study the working of the LBS in Gujarat and Maharashtra, as per the decision taken in the Regional Consultative Committee (Western Region) held in August 1975. A common report was submitted by the group in December 1975, in view of the similarity of the problems. The group made several important recommendations, regarding composition and functioning of DCCs, training needs of the staff of banks and state governments, constitution of a standing committee in RBI for reviewing the overall progress of LBS etc. The "High Power Committee on the working of LBS" was constituted by RBI in 1976, as per the recommendation of the Committee. As rapid branch expansion had taken place by then, the group recommended implementation of the next phase of the LBS viz., formulation and implementation of area development programme, covering activities in priority sectors to fill the sectoral credit gap. This marked the beginning of a crucial phase in LBS.

**District Credit Plan (DCP)**

The second and most important phase of the LBS was formulation of Credit plans (CPs) and their implementation. Although certain structural credit gaps were identified earlier, positive measures were introduced only after nationalization of the banks. Certain sectors, which were hitherto neglected, were given a priority status and banks were asked to provide credit to these sectors in a more concerted way. Priority sector included agriculture, small scale industries (SSI), small road and water transport operators, retail trade and small business, education, self-employed persons etc. It was made mandatory for the Credit plans to deploy a stipulated percentage of credit for priority sector. It was fixed at 33.30 per cent of the outstanding credit by March 1979 and 40 per cent by March 1985. Within the priority sector, sub-targets were prescribed for agriculture and allied activities and weaker sections. The credit planning exercise under the LBS, primarily, aimed at overall development of a district, through the coordinated efforts of banks, acting in unison with the developmental organs of the State Government at the district level. The first set of DCPs were prepared and launched in 1978. In the second round of DCPs (1980-82) further refinements were made. The credit outlays, under DCPs, were now required to be prepared, not merely sector-wise but also bank-wise and block-wise. Besides, within the plan period, outlays were required to be worked out annually to be Annual Action Plans (AAP) for each block, bank and sector/sub-sector. The third (1983-85) and fourth round (1988-90) of DCPs and AAPs further contributed to the familiarity of banks in the mechanism of credit planning. The cooperatives were also involved in the preparation of DCPs. They too were allotted their share of targets under priority sector/Government sponsored programmes.

**Standing Committee of DCC**

A task force comprising representatives of DCCs, Commercial Banks (CBs) having wide network of branches in the district and District Planning Officials was set up, to assist the lead bank in the preparation of operationally meaningful DCP and AAP. This task force was converted into a Standing Committee of DCC for associating it in the implementation of the plans. Its membership was enlarged to include the Lead District Officer (LDO) of RBI, representative of ARDC (now District Development Managers DDM, NABARD), the Chief Executive of DRDA/(Zilla Parishads also) and an official from the Co-operative Department.

**Lead Bank Officers and Lead District Officers**

The organizational base of the Lead Banks was strengthened for preparation of DCPs and for their monitoring and implementation. RBI advised them in 1979, to appoint a Lead Bank Officer normally called Lead District Manager (LDM) in each district for the purpose. Our Lead Banks are being headed by Lead District Managers. Simultaneously, RBI appointed LDOs who were allotted 4 or 5 districts each and were entrusted with the responsibilities of overseeing the preparation and implementation of DCPs in the allotted districts.

### Village Adoption Scheme (VAS)

Concomitant to LBS, the other form of area approach in operation was VAS, under which banks adopted some villages in their command area, for intensive lending. The area approach was not so much aimed at development of a chosen area as for avoiding the pitfalls of scattered and unsupervised lending. In the initial stages of VAS, RBI encouraged banks to adopt villages as well as to avoid scattered lending. A study carried out by the RBI in 1980 revealed, that the VAS, in practice, mainly served to exclude other banks from going to the adopted villages of one bank for financing, without ensuring that the branch adopting the villages, paid adequate attention for meeting their credit needs. The RBI, therefore, issued guidelines in December 1980, spelling out that adoption of villages by a bank, essentially, should have an intention to intensify its efforts therein and should not mean that other banks are precluded from financing in the area.

### Emergence of Regional Rural Banks

Nationalisation of banks was not able to bridge the entire credit gap in the rural areas. A vast majority of the small and marginal farmers and rural artisans remained untouched by the banking system. Therefore, the range of institutional alternatives was widened in 1975 by adding Regional Rural Banks (RRBs) to the banking scene which would exclusively cater to the credit demands of the hitherto neglected segment of the rural economy. Thus, with Co-operatives, Commercial Banks and RRBs, a multi-agency approach was adopted in the rural credit system.

### Emergence of Service Area Approach

There was a need to have a close look at the quality of lending by banks. It has been observed that during the five years 1981-86, the gross value, added in agricultural sector, registered a growth rate of 2.70 per cent per annum. The share of agriculture in the total net domestic product at factor cost declined from 39.80 per cent to 35.40 per cent. The production of food grains increased, marginally, from 133.30

million tones to 150.50 million tones, an increase of 18 per cent with considerable regional disparities. The rate of growth in the consumption of fertilizers was also similar. In contrast, there was 41 per cent increase in the outstanding level of credit for agriculture from all the three rural lending agencies namely Co-operatives, RRBs and CBs between June 1981 and June 1986.

State-wise comparison of production of foodgrains vis-à-vis outstanding bank credit showed wide disparities. The share of Haryana, Punjab and Uttra pradesh in total foodgrain production was around 38 per cent. These states accounted for as much as 75 per cent increase in the foodgrain output. However, their share in the total institutional credit was 22 per cent only. While some of the states in the Eastern Region and Madhya Pradesh have done well in recent years, stagnation or decline in foodgrain production was noticed in Himachal Pradesh, Rajasthan, Gujarat, Maharashtra, Andhra Pradesh, Karnataka and Kerala which account for 41 per cent of the area under cultivation of food crops and comparatively a high proportion of institutional credit for agriculture.

In the context of these variations, taking into account the massive increase in rural lending, as also the further increase in such credit deployment in the years to come, it was considered opportune to assess the impact which credit from banks has had on the overall economic development of the rural sector, in general and agricultural production and in productivity, in particular, through an indepth study.

With this objective in view, the Governor of RBI suggested to the Chief executives of Public Sector Banks, in a meeting held on 17.10.1987 that a field study should be carried out in different districts all over the country. Accordingly, studies were conducted in 88 districts spread over 21 states in November/December 1987and reports were submitted to RBI. The findings of the field studies were discussed in a seminar convened by RBI on 9th and 10th January 1988. It was attended by the Chairman of Public Sector Banks, top executives from the Government of India and the national level institutions. Honorable Finance Minister and Minister of State for Finance addressed the Seminar.

The findings of these studies revealed a major deficiency in the rural credit system viz., a weak link between bank credit and production, productivity and income levels. Scattered lending over wide areas diluted the quality of lending. Post-disbursement supervision was paid little or no attention. Several suggestions were made at the seminar for strengthening the existing rural credit delivery system with a view to improving the quality of lending in rural areas. The most important suggestion by all the participants was the endorsement of the new approach to rural lending viz., SERVICE AREA APPROACH, whereby each rural and semi-urban branch of a commercial bank (including RRB) would be assigned a designated area, in which it could make planned efforts towards area development in co-ordination with all the extension and development agencies of the State Government. Large scale expansion of branches in rural and semi-urban areas facilitated the shift.

The suggestion was formalized when the Union Finance Minister announced in his budget speech on 29th February 1988 about the new scheme. The operational aspects of implementing this approach were examined in depth, by a Committee appointed for the purpose under the Chairmanship of Dr. P.D. Ojha, Deputy Governor of RBI. The members of the Committee, among others were the Chairman of some public sector banks. In the absence of sufficient knowledge about the potential within the command area, these targets tended to be unrealistic.

## Important Recommendations of Dr. Ojha Committee

The Committee opined that the Lead Bank Scheme has helped in bringing a great deal of co-ordination between banks and Government departments through forums established at the district and state level, but as the district development plans and branch performance budgets could not be dovetailed with the DCPs and AAPs prepared under the scheme, and hence they could not acquire the full status of operationally relevant plans for implementation. The lack of involvement of Branch Mangers in the preparation of plans was also responsible for the plans not becoming meaningful to them. Under these circumstances, an alternative system, as suggested in the Seminar, appears to be more conducive to develop productive lending.

The issue of demarcation of area, as advocated by the working group on multi-agency approach on Agricultural Finance, was formalized with the advent of SAA. The committee also expressed that such an approach would have distinct advantages in the dispensation of credit. Firstly, it enables the branches to pay concentrated attention on the development of the area. Secondly, as the multi-agency approach has, to some extent, resulted in duplication of efforts, a new approach may help in avoiding the same. Thirdly, the scattered lending over wide areas would give way to organised lending. Fourthly, it would make it easier for the branch managers to effectively monitor the end-use of credit and assess the impact on increase in the levels of production, productivity and income of the beneficiaries. Finally, as the plans would be drawn up by the branch manager, he would develop a sense of pride, motivation and involvement in the success of these plans.

## STATE LEVEL BANKERS' COMMITTEE (SLBC)

The State Level Bankers' Committee (SLBC) is an inter-institutional forum for co-ordination and joint implementation of development programmes and policies, by all the financial institutions operating in a State. Although SLBC is envisaged as a Bankers' forum, Government officials are also included. The Committee is expected to discuss issues, consider alternative solutions to the various problems in the field of balanced development and evolve a consensus for coordinated action by the member institutions. All the member institutions, are therefore, expected to approach the Committee's task in a spirit of co-ordination and intimate involvement without which the Committee is likely to lose its utility.

These committees are to consider all problems requiring inter-bank coordination at the policy and implementation level. SLBCs are also expected to recommend to the state government, measures which would facilitate intensive involvement of banks and effective co-ordination with extension agencies for all-round banking development.

The SLBC is constituted by the following persons:

**Chairman:** The chairman of the Convener Bank. If he is not available due to unavoidable circumstances, Executive Director of the Bank.

**Convener:** The Lead Bank designated as 'Convener Bank'

**Members**

- Representative of RBI
- Representative of NABARD
- Representative of IDBI
- Representative of SIDBI
- Representative of IFCI
- Representative of all Lead Banks in the State
- Representative of other banks, having a fair network of branches in the rural, semi-urban and urban areas of the state.
- Representative of State Co-operative Bank
- Representative of State Land Development Bank
- Representative of State Financial Corporation
- Representative of RRBs
- The concerned Secretary/Director of Institutional Finance of State Government
- The representative of departments of State Government connected with rural development

- The Planning Secretary of State Government
- Representatives of other banks may be invited to specific meetings of SLBC, wherever considered necessary.

**Invitees**

- Representative of National Commission for SC/STs
- Chairman/Managing Director of State Minority Communities/Boards or the State Minorities Financial Corporation or a representative

The Regional Rural Bank would be represented by the Chairman. Banks having less than 5 branches in a state could, however, be represented by the manger of the branch of the bank, located at State Headquarters. RBI vide RPCD LBS 97/02.01.01/2003-04 dt. 23.03.2003, has reiterated that banks having sizeable scale of operations in the State, are expected to be represented in the SLBC meetings at the level of Zonal/Regional Managers, so that expeditious decision-making becomes possible. Convener Bank may ensure this by taking up the matter with RBI, where the level of participation is below the stipulated level. In the case of State Governments, senior functionaries are expected to attend the SLBC meetings.

**Functions of the SLBC**

1. To discuss issues, consider alternative solutions to the various problems in the filed of banking development and evolve consensus for coordinated action by the member institutions.
2. To do the necessary spadework for formulation of Annual Credit Plans for getting in the district-wise resource allocation by banks and desegregations of the various Government programmes.
3. To examine the inter-institutional co-ordination in the formulation and implementation of the Annual Credit Plans.
4. To undertake critical analysis of the progress of the implementation of Annual Credit Plans and Government/

Other agencies' sponsored credit-linked programmes/ schemes in the various districts.

5. To review the assistance required and provided by Government agencies.
6. To consider problems, referred by the district level forums and take necessary follow-up action.
7. To oversee the implementation of branch expansion programme.
8. To review the recovery performance.
9. To ensure arrangements for training of both bank and government staff as well as evaluation of the programmes implemented.
10. To take up for consideration such issues as have been raised by the member banks and/or the State Government authorities and questions or inter-bank differences remaining unresolved at the District Level Consultative Committees.
11. To solve operational problems in the implementation of Service Area Approach, Credit Plans, Government and other agencies' programmes, etc. To discuss about the availability of adequate infrastructural facilities, forward and backward linkages necessary for successful implementation of the schemes.
12. To serve as a focal point for the banking system in the state for securing better liaison with the State Government authorities.
13. To review the trends in the flow of credit into rural areas and to the small borrowers in the neglected sectors.
14. To purposefully review the picture revealed by the data compiled, in accordance with the system of returns and take follow-up measures for the speedy disposal of loan applications, to improve the pace of credit assistance under specific programmes/schemes of the Central Government such as PMRY, SGSY, SJSRY, SLRS,SC/ST action plan and all state sponsored schemes.

15. To review Credit Deposit Ratio, priority sector advances, advances to weaker section, financing of minority communities etc.
16. To review performance under Self-Help Groups, Kisan Credit Cards, Crop Insurance Scheme, Laghu Udyami Credit Cards, Swarozgar Credit Cards, Artisan Credit Cards etc.
17. To undertake/entrust study of any specific problems in implementation of Lead Bank Scheme, Service Area Approach, Development Programmes etc, by appointing 'Study Groups' and by involving Government departments, more intimately concerned with the problem and having greater expertise at their command.
18. To review the progress made in achieving the targets set under the various schemes.
19. To liaise with the representative of State Level Association of SSI for promoting SSI.
20. Confirming/ratifying the action initiated by the Steering Committee of SLBC.

**Functions of the Convener Bank**

- To maintain co-ordination in the functioning of different financial institutions, operating in the State, in the implementation of various developmental programmes (both Central and State).
- To consider problems, requiring inter-bank co-ordination, matters relating to banking development etc, requiring state level attention.
- To conduct SLBC meetings, Steering Committee meetings and annual SLRM, depending upon the requirement.
- To take up for consideration, the issues raised by member banks and the State authorities, which remain unresolved in the District Consultative Committees (DCCs)/ District Level Review Committee meetings (DLRCs).
- To serve as a focal point for the banking system, as a whole, in the State in order to secure better liaison with

the state government authorities and apex institutions like RBI/NABARD/SIDBI etc.

- To disseminate guidelines and policy matters to all the member banks and others concerned, regularly.
- To allocate targets, in co-ordination with State Government, under different government sponsored schemes.
- To collect and consolidate feed-back reports from Banks/ State Government departments and Lead District Managers for preparing agenda notes for SLBC/Steering Committee/SLRM.
- To attend State Level Meetings convened by various departments/ organizations, on behalf of Banks as Convener of SLBC and to initiate necessary follow up thereof.

**Role of the Convener**

1. Obtaining necessary background notes and data from financial institutions, Government departments, Lead Bank Officers at district level and other agencies, to prepare comprehensive agenda notes for SLBC meeting.
2. Convening the meeting by issuing notice and sending agenda and agenda notes to the members sufficiently in advance, say, 15 days in minimum.
3. Suggest matters for discussion.
4. Convene Steering Committee meetings.
5. Recording the proceedings of the meeting.
6. Circulating the minutes to the members of SLBC, all Banks, financial institutions and Government departments etc, within a fortnight.
7. Following action points arising out of discussions and decisions.
8. Referring the unresolved problems at SLBC meeting to the RBI/GOI/State Government, for taking up at the appropriate level. Holding periodical discussions at Government/RBI level to resolve pending issues.

9. Reviewing the list of member invitees on a continuous basis.
10. To ensure that steps are taken to facilitate the flow of credit to the Minority Communities, SC/STs and Weaker sections and the progress made in this regard are reviewed regularly at the meetings.
11. Taking up the matter with RBI and Heads of the Banks/ Agencies for non-participation/junior level participation.
12. To liaise with the SLBC Conveners of other states for exchange of ideas best practices.

**Periodicity of Meetings**

Each State Level Bankers' Committee may meet, as often as necessary, keeping in view the business on hand. It is, however, expected that the frequency of such meetings will in no case be less than once every quarter.

It is expected that the nominated representatives of the banks, will attend all the meetings of the main committee, the Steering Committee or any Study Group. If for any unavoidable reason, a nominated representative of a bank cannot be present at any particular meeting, he should nominate his next in command, to attend the meeting on his behalf, after duly briefing him about the bank's views on the various items of the agenda for that meeting. The objective should be that issues for considerations do not get postponed for want of attendance of the representatives of the banks.

**Proceedings of the Meetings and Follow up Action**

The proceedings of the meetings of the Committee or its Sub-Committee may be drawn up by the Convener Bank and circulated to all the members, within a fortnight of the date of the meeting. Each bank is expected to initiate follow-up action, on the consensus arrived at the meetings of the Committee. Endeavour should be made to implement all the recommendations of the Committee.

The Convener Bank may present to the Committee an assessment report of the follow up action taken by the banks on the decisions of the Committee. No acceptance of/non-compliance with the recommendations of the Committee may be specifically listed in such reports.

**Scope Activities**

The State Level Bankers' Committee is expected to take up for consideration such issues as have been raised by the member banks or by the State Government authorities and questions or inter-bank difference on views and approach, remaining unresolved at the District-Level Consultative Committees. While all the State Level Banker's Committees are, thus, expected to address themselves to the problems particular to the concerned state, some of the problem areas which are expected to be common to all the states and which many of the State Level Bankers' Committees have already taken up or decided to take up for consideration, are briefly enumerated below:

**1. Regional imbalances in availability of banking facilities**

Not withstanding the growth of the banking system, there are large geographical areas which continue to be devoid of banking branches. Government has already advised the SLBCs to draw up an agreed programme of branch expansion so as to provide each unbanked community development block, with atleast one commercial bank branch. Besides evolving co-ordinated programmes to secure this objective and overseeing their implementation, the SLBCs are expected to review the spread of branch network so as to ensure that branches are equitably dispersed throughout the state and important development centres such as block headquarters etc., do not remain unserved and in under-banked states/districts, bank services do not remain limited to district headquarters alone but spread into rural areas.

**2. Regional imbalances in deployment of credit**

In the sphere of deployment of credit also, there are severe imbalances. SLBCs are to concentrate in stepping up of credit deployment in those districts, where the credit deposit ratio is less than the State/National average. SLBCs are expected to review the credit deployment position in their respective states and consciously evolve programmes for improving it, where it is unsatisfactory.

### 3. Area demarcation for effective coverage

While in relation to the credit requirements of the neglected sectors, the quantum of institutional credit constitutes only a small percentage, multiplicities of credit agencies in specific pockets seem to have created problems of overlapping in areas. This leads to dual financing by different institutions and a certain dilution of institutional responsibility. The SLBCs are expected to address themselves in this task. The pattern of existing coverage could be ascertained from the member institutions and areas of overlapping as also of total neglect, be identified. In relation to the former, the concerned institutions could sit together and arrive at an agreed area of operation for each of them. In relation to the latter, the Committee will have to consider ways and means of extending coverage. Such areas would also indicate the manner in which further branch expansion need to be reoriented.

Banks are also participating in a number of schemes, sponsored by the state governments. They are also participating in programmes, which form part of the District Credit Plans formulated by the Lead Banks. Area allocation among different participating institutions would have an important bearing on the overall progress of the schemes. State-level Bankers' Committee is expected to ensure that specific schemes/programmes are properly allocated amongst participating institutions so that the implementation does not suffer because of dilution of responsibility, implicit in overlapping operational areas.

### 4. Liaison with state governments

The SLBC is expected to serve as a focal point for the Banking System in every state, for securing better liaison with

State Government authorities. The State Governments have been advised of the constitution of these committees and it is desired that the Convener Banks approach the State Government authorities and apprise them of the activities of these Committees.

**5. Review of the functioning of district consultative committees**

The State Level Bankers' Committees, Such problems should be brought before the committee by the Lead Banks concerned. Agreed decisions could, then, be communicated by all the participating institutions to their respective field for action, in the concerned districts.

**6. District Credit Plans (DCP)**

Inter-institutional co-ordination is of critical importance in the formulation and implementation of the District Credit Plans. This aspect may, therefore, be regularly examined by the SLBCs. Allocation of shares in the District Credit Plans should invariably be ratified by the Regional/Zonal Managers of the Banks, participating in the district plans concerned. This would ensure extending necessary support to the branches in the implementation of plans. Progress reports on the implementation of the plans are expected to be prepared every six months. The State Level Bankers' Committee may review these reports and ensure appropriate follow-up action to see that plan implementation is in accordance with the envisaged time- schedule.

**7. Uniformity in terms and conditions of lending**

While the terms and conditions, governing the advances, are determined by each bank, keeping in view various factors such as cost of mobilising resources, operational costs, security requirements etc., wide variations in these conditions from bank to bank, creates confusion and resentment in the minds of the borrowers especially several institutions are participating. If at least, in respect of advances to be granted under specific schemes the banks strive to achieve certain uniformity in terms and conditions governing their advances. Two specific elements, wherein variations have a direct impact on the borrowers, are the scale of finance and the rate of interest. Therefore, at least in respect of specific schemes, the State Level Bankers' committees could endeavor to evolve scales of finance and rates of interest, which all the banks participating in the specific schemes could adopt.

### 8. Review of credit flows

The State Level Bankers' Committees could become a very useful forum for reviewing the trends in the flow of credit into rural areas and to the small borrowers in the neglected sectors. An important prerequisite for such reviews is the availability of data. Recently, a system of statistical reporting for the use of the District Level Consultative and the State Level Co-ordination Committees, evolved by a Study Group, has been introduced. The State Level Bankers' Committees could also purposefully review the picture revealed by the data, compiled in accordance with the new system of returns and take follow-up measures to secure speedy disposal of loan applications and to improve the pace of credit assistance under specific programmes.

Government has advised the Banks to consciously endeavour to step up the flow of credit in rural areas. To start with, they have been advised to secure a credit deposit ratio of at least 60 per cent in respect of their rural and semi-urban branches, separately. Progress in this direction, in each State could be kept under constant observation, by the State Level Bankers' Committees.

## STEERING COMMITTEE OF SLBC

The Steering Committee is a sub-committee of SLBC. The membership of SLBC, often, may be too large to permit effective deliberations, maintenance of liaison and decision-making. Therefore, this sub-committee is constituted at State level, to go into each issue in depth.

The Steering Sub-Committee may be constituted as under:

**Chairman:** Zonal Head of Convener Bank/Any other Leading Bank Manager.

**Convener:** The Lead Bank designated as 'Convener Bank'

**Members**

- Representative of RBI
- Representative of NABARD
- Representative of IDBI
- Representative of SIDBI
- Representative of IFCI
- Representative of all Lead Banks in the State
- Representative of other banks, having a fair network of branches in the rural, semi-urban and urban areas of the state, as decided by the SLBC.
- Representative of State Co-operative Bank
- Representative of State Land Development Bank
- Representative of State Financial Corporation
- Chairman of RRBs
- The concerned Secretary/Director of Institutional Finance of State Government
- The Planning Secretary of State Government (The representatives of the commercial banks in the Steering Sub-Committee may not be below the rank of Region/ Zonal Managers).

**Periodicity of Meetings**

The 'Steering Committee' should meet more often than the main Committee. It would, however, be helpful if the State Level Bankers' Committees do meet and discuss issues, before every meeting of the State Level Co-ordination Committees, so as to facilitate the banks to take an innovative and co-ordinated view of the problems, proposed to be discussed by the State Level Co-ordination Committees.

## Functions of the Steering Committee

1. To review/follow-up/sort out various issues/action points emerging from the meeting of SLBC.
2. Discuss in detail, fresh issues referred to the SLBC and record the views and refer appropriate items to SLBC with recommendations/views.
3. To follow up periodically, the implementation of various Government-sponsored schemes/programmes.
4. To monitor the progress in the field of formulation of new schemes.
5. To ascertain the problems, in implementing the schemes and suggest solutions, and
6. To do the necessary spade work for SLBC meeting, including screening of the agenda items.

## Role of the Convener

1. Collect items/issues for discussion, by sending a communication to all the members of SLBC.
2. Brief the Standing Committee on follow-up action taken and recommendations of SLBC.
3. Suggest items suo-moto for discussion, if necessary.
4. Preparing agenda notes for the meeting in a systematic way.
5. Convening the meeting by issuing notice and agenda notes well in advance, say, 15 days.
6. Recording the proceedings of the meeting.
7. Circulating the minutes to the members of the Committee, all Banks, financial institutions and Government departments etc within a fortnight of the meeting.
8. Following up the action points arising out of discussions and decisions.

## STATE LEVEL CONSULTATIVE COMMITTEE (SLCC)

This is a committee constituted by the State Government to review the performance of banks in assisting credit-based development programmes taken up by the State Government Meetings are convened by the State Government.

This committee is constituted as under:

**Chairman:** The Chief Minister/Finance Minister of the State

**Convener:** The Secretary/Director of Institutional Finance (providing necessary secretarial assistance)

**Members**

- The Chief Secretary
- Director of Institutional Finance of State Government
- Senior State Government officials, viz., Departmental Secretaries, Registrar of Cooperative Societies etc.
- Representative of RBI
- Representative of NABARD, SIDBI and IDBI
- Representative of SBI & other Lead Banks
- Representative of State Co-operative Banks
- Representative of Convener Bank of State Level Committee of RRBs. (The representatives of banks may not be below the level of General Managers).

**Periodicity of meeting** - Once a year

## STANDING COMMITTEE OF SLCC

The Standing Committee of SLCC is a sub-committee of SLCC, constituted to provide a compact form of co-ordination between financial agencies and Government departments. Meetings are convened by the State Government.

The Standing committee is constituted as under:

**Chairman:** The Chief Secretary/Finance Secretary/ Development Commissioner

**Convener:** The Secretary/Director of Institutional Finance (providing necessary secretarial assistance)

**Members**

- Representative of all Lead Banks in the State.

- Representative of Convener Bank of State Level Committee of RRBs.
- Representative of RBI
- Representative of NABARD
- Representative of SIDBI/IDBI
- Representative of State Co-operative Bank
- Representative of State Land Development Bank
- Representative of concerned development departments of the Government. (Total strength should be around 20 and at very senior level).

**Periodicity of meeting** - Once in 3 months

**Functions of the Standing Committee**

1. To do the spadework for ACP formulation by furnishing well in time, estimates of district-wise disaggregation of governmental development programmes needing credit support, with financial outlays regarding subsidies etc.
2. To monitor proper phasing of such schemes, taking into account availability of necessary linkages and optimal levels of implementation.
3. To provide infrastructural and extension facilities and other supporting measures required from governmental agencies.
4. To assess the qualitative aspects of the Bank, lending under the various schemes.
5. To monitor the trend in the growth of deposits, advances, sectoral flow of credit etc.
6. To monitor the functioning of various levels of co-ordination machinery.
7. Arranging training programmes for bank and government staff.
8. Review of recovery performance including legislative and administrative support required from government.

9. Arrangements for evaluation area-wise, activity-wise institutions wise etc.

## STATE LEVEL REVIEW MEETING (SLRM)

### Objectives

1. To review the performance of the Banking Industry in lending to Priority Sectors and Weaker Section vis-a-vis National goals i.e. the norms stipulated by the Government of India/RBI.
2. To review the achievements under ACP/DCP and to suggest strategies for enhancing flow of credit to priority sector.
3. To review the progress in the implementation of programmes like SGSY, PMRY, SJSRY, SHG and other State Government Sponsored Schemes.
4. To discuss the operational problems/issues faced by Banks in the implementation of various schemes and to improve flow of information through returns from Banks under Lead Bank Scheme.

Keeping the above issues in the background, the relevant issues/topics selected are discussed in the preliminary meeting of subject-wise groups, constituted for this purpose and the recommendations of the Group are presented/placed before SLRM/SLBC for adoption. The SLRM provides an opportunity to find out/identify the reasons coming in the way of implementation of various programmes/schemes and also to suggest solutions/strategies, through collective discussion for successful implementation.

## DISTRICT CONSULTATIVE COMMITTEE (DCC)

The DCC has been constituted at the instance of Banking Commission (1972) and is a common forum for bankers as well as Government officials to find solutions to problems, in implementing schemes under LBS. The DCC came into existence more or less voluntarily because of the need felt for consultation in the matter of District Development Schemes. Over the years, it has evolved as an integral part of the LBS.

The DCC is constituted as under:

**Chairman:** District Collector/Deputy Commissioner

**Convener:** Lead District Manger

**Members**

- Chief Executive Officer, ZP
- District Planning Officer
- Project Director for DRDA
- General Manager, DIC
- Executive Officer, State SC and BC Corporations, District Level functionaries of Agriculture, Veterinary, Animal Husbandary, Sericulture, Fisheries and Irrigation dept etc.
- Lead District Officer, RBI
- Representative of NABARD
- Regional Managers/District Coordinators of 5 or 6 commercial banks, having a large commitment under credit plan, priority sector lending and branch network
- Representative of RRB
- District representatives of State Financial Corporation KVIC and KVIB
- Representatives of District Central Co-operative Bank and other Co-operative Banks, having a large commitment under credit plans.

Other government departments, Corporations, Boards, Universities and Banks, which are not permanent members, may be invited to attend specific meetings, whenever considered necessary, on the basis of agenda items. Each member should be represented only by one official of an appropriate level at DCC meeting. The overall strength of DCC should be maintained at a compact level of 20 to 25 members so that the discussions at this forum are meaningful and result oriented.

**Periodicity of meeting:** Once in 3 months.

## Functions

1. Identification of potential and formulation of bankable schemes.
2. Finalisation of Annual District Credit Plan, based on the block plans approved by BLBCs.
3. Allocation of physical and financial targets of various government and other agencies' credit-linked programmes/schemes to the financial institution in the district.
4. Monitoring the overall progress/performance in physical and financial terms of the implementation of ACP, Government-sponsored Schemes and all other programmes/schemes.
5. To solve the operational problems in the implementation of Service Area Approach, Credit Plans, Government and other agencies' programmes/schemes etc.
6. Reviewing/Monitoring of the support forthcoming from Government Departments.
7. Identifying problems/bottlenecks in provision of credit as also of infrastructure, inputs etc and taking steps to overcome these.
8. Reviewing bank-wise and sector/activity-wise position of credit disbursement under ACP and Government and other agencies' programmes/schemes etc and initiating necessary action.
9. Reviewing the progress in disposal of loan applications and ensuring that applications are sent in a phased manner and not bunched together in the last quarter of the financial year.
10. Overseeing and ensuring smooth release of subsidies.
11. Monitoring the recovery position of financial agencies and rendering necessary help for recovery of overdues.
12. Taking up with the State Government/SLBC/SLCC, items/issues which cannot be tackled at the district level and ensuring proper follow up thereof.

13. Consideration of security arrangements and other infrastructural facilities for rural branches.
14. Evaluation of the ground level implementation of various schemes and benefits accruing there of to the identified beneficiaries.
15. Monitoring the position in regard to Credit Deposit ratio (CD Ratio) in the light of RBI stipulations in this regard.
16. Discussing the follow-up of DLRC's decisions.
17. Identifying activities/programmes/schemes suited to local circumstances.
18. Recommending to SLBC to request the State Government to devise suitable polices for inputs, services and marketing and in- building suitable supporting organizations for all the three items.
19. To deliberate on broad planning and operational aspects and not to deal with individual cases.
20. To review Credit Deposit Ratio, priority sector advances, advances to weaker section etc.
21. Confirming/ratifying the action initiated by the Standing Committee.

**Functions of the Convener**

1. Obtaining necessary background notes and data from financial institutions, Government departments and other agencies to prepare comprehensive agenda notes for DCC meeting.
2. Convening the meeting by issuing notice and agenda notes to the members sufficiently in advance, say, 15 days.
3. Recording the proceedings of the meeting. The proceedings should bring out clearly the discussions and decisions arrived at. The agencies responsible for taking further action on the decisions, together with the time schedule for such action, should be indicated in the proceedings. The concerned agencies should provide necessary feedback to DCC, regarding the action taken

on the decisions. The items not advised before hand, but raised in the meeting should be listed separately in the proceedings.

4. Circulating minutes to the member of DCC, all banks, financial institutions and Government departments etc., within a fortnight.
5. Following up issues requiring action by banks, other financial agencies and Government departments.
6. To act as resource person for the entire banking sector, in the lead district, so far as the implementations of credit plan is concerned.
7. While ensuring that DCC becomes a compact forum for meaningful discussions, it is necessary to secure an arrangement for adequate rapport between DCC and those institutions which are not represented in it, on a permanent basis. The LDM should function as the focal point of such co-ordination by convening regularly, meetings with the District co-ordinators of all non-lead banks and other financial institutions. These meetings should be held well in advance of DCC meetings so that the problems thrown up could be taken up at the DCC forum. LDOs of RBI and representative of NABARD may also be invited for such meetings.

## STANDING COMMITTEE OF DCC (SC)

The guidelines issued by the RBI, for the formulation of DCPs during 1980-82 on a uniform basis, envisaged the constitutions of Task Force of bankers and planning officials at the district level. The task force became a permanent body and evolved into Standing Committee (SC). The Standing Committee of DCC is a small subcommittee of the DCC, constituted to attend to all important matters relating to implementation of the District Credit Plan on an ongoing basis.

The SC is constituted as under:

**Chairman:** District Collector/Deputy Commissioner

**Convener:** Lead District Manager

**Members**

- Chief Executive Officer, Zilla Parishad (ZP)
- District Planning Officer
- Project Director, DRDA
- General Manager, DIC
- Executive Officers, Ståte SC/BC Corporations
- District Development Manager (DDM/NABARD)
- Lead District Officer, RBI
- District Coordinators of 2 or 3 major commercial (non-lead) banks, who have a large net work of branches and large lendings, under Government sponsored schemes/ programmes.

  **Periodicity of meeting:** Once in a month excepting the month in which DCC/DLRC is held.

**Functions**

The functions of the Standing Committee inter alia, cover the following:

1. To make indepth studies of the development, potential in the blocks/district.
2. To evolve economically-viable and technically-feasible schemes.
3. To collect relevant data for formulating credit plans and finalise scale of finance of various crops cultivated in the district.
4. To prepare bankable schemes.
5. To review implementation of credit plans and other agencies sponsored credit-linked programmes/schemes sponsored by the Government.
6. To sort out grass root-level operational problems and take them to DCC, where consensus for solutions could be arrived at.

7. To prepare background note for DCC meeting.

**Functions of the Convener**

1. Preparing the agenda notes for the meeting.
2. Convening the monthly meeting by issuing notice and agenda notes well in advance.
3. Recording the proceedings of the meeting and circulating the minutes to the members, all banks, financial institutions and Government departments etc., within a fortnight.
4. Following up the action points with the concerned banks/ Government agencies.

## DISTRICT LEVEL REVIEW COMMITTEE (DLRC)

The DLRC is a larger body of DCC, constituted for discussing, in detail, the different aspects of the LBS/ Implementation of District Credit Plan under each sector viz., Agriculture, Industries and Services, identify problems and involve remedial steps.

The DLRC is constituted as below:

**Chairman:** District Collector/Deputy Commissioner

**Convener:** Lead District Manager

**Members**

- Chief Executive Officer, Zilla Parishad (ZP)
- District Planning Officer
- Project Director, DRDA
- General Manager, DIC
- Executive Officers, State SC/BC Corporations
- Representative of NABARD/District Development Manager
- Lead District Officer, RBI
- Regional Managers/District Coordinators of all commercial banks, who implement credit plan under Lead Bank Scheme.

- Representative of RBI.
- District representative of State Financial Corporation, KVIC, KVIB.
- Representatives of District Central Cooperative Bank and other Co-operative Banks who implement credit plan under LBS.

**Association of Non-officials**

Two non-officials, who are in close or intimate association with critical sectors of development like agriculture, small scale industry, tribal development and Harijan Welfare Development.

**Peoples' representatives** : All local MPs and MLAs.

**Periodicity of meeting** : Quarterly

**Functions of the Non-officials**

1. Evaluating the progress made in the implementation of schemes/activities, under each sector viz., Agriculture, Industries and Services, included in the Annual District Credit Plan, identifying problems and devising suitable remedial steps by forming separate sectoral groups.
2. Reviewing the progress made in the field of special programmes like PMRY, SGSY, SJSRY etc.
3. Discussing the suggestions made by sectoral groups in the plenary session of DLRC meeting and arriving at conclusions for follow-up and their implementation and fixing responsibilities for resolving the problems.
4. Reviewing the progress in co-ordination, problems relating to overdues/recoveries and Government support, infrastructure facilities available/to be provided, functioning of DIC etc.

**Functions of the Convener**

1. Identifying the activities/schemes, included in Annual Credit Plan, the progress/performance of which is not encouraging and putting up the same to sectoral groups for discussion and devising suitable remedial steps.

2. Obtaining necessary back-ground notes and data from financial institutions, government departments and other agencies to prepare comprehensive agenda notes for DLRC meeting.
3. Convening the meeting by sending notice and agenda notes to the members sufficiently in advance, say, 15 days.
4. Recording the proceedings of the meeting.
5. Circulating minutes to the member of DLRC within a fortnight.
6. Following up issues/decisions, requiring action by banks, other financial agencies and Government departments.

## BLOCK LEVEL BANKERS' COMMITTEE (BLBC)

Block Level Bankers' Committee is a body, comprising of development departments, headed by Block Development Officer and Branch Mangers of all the branches of the Block. The BLBC is constituted for discussing, in detail, the different aspects of the Lead Bank Scheme/implementation of the Credit Plan and to review the progress in the implementation of the various government-sponsored Schemes.

The BLBC is constituted as below:

**Chairman:** Lead District Manager.

**Convener:** Branch Manager of the Branch of the Lead Bank in the block headquarters. In case, the Lead bank has no branch in the block headquarters then the Branch Manager of the bank having major share in the branch network with branch in the block, head quarters will be designated for the same.

**Members**

- Block Development Officer
- Technical Officers (Agriculture)
- Technical Officer (Industries)
- Technical Officer (Animal Husbandry)

- Branch Manager of all Commercial Banks, Regional Rural Banks, District Central Co-operative Banks and Land Development Banks
- Lead District Officer of RBI, wherever possible
- DDM of NABARD, wherever possible.

**Periodicity of meeting** - Quarterly

The joint forum for consultation and monitoring of DCPs, under LBS, had been created only upto district level and not block level. But some of the states governments had set up block-level committees or Task Forces for monitoring implementation of special programme like SGSY, SJSRY, PMRY, SLRS, 20 Point Programme etc. Commercial banks extend necessary co-operation and participate in the discussion but do not convene the meetings/act as conveners this being done by BDO in some states. State governments have advised that meetings may be held in the Block and Branch premises alternatively to invoke better co-operation. Matters of policy issues and cases of individual borrowers are not discussed / decided in such meetings but are referred to higher officials/ DCC.

However, with the adoption of service area approach, RBI has advised formation of a Block-Level Bankers' Committee (BLBC), to co-ordinate the activities of the banks and the government officials. All the banks operating in the block, including DCCB, LDB and RRB, would be members of this committee. In addition, the Block Development Officer and the Technical officers in the block, looking after agriculture, industries, animal husbandry etc, would also be the members. The Lead Bank Officer of the concerned district would be the Chairman of the Committee and in his absence, the senior-most branch manager of the lead bank would preside over the meeting and he would also work as its Convener. If the Lead Bank has no branch in the block, as stated earlier, another bank which has maximum presence in the block and designated by the Lead Bank, shall act as the Convener. The Lead District Officer of the Reserve Bank of

India and the concerned officer from NABARD, should draw up definite programmes enabling either of them to attend the block-level meeting.

**Functions**

1. To discuss the credit plans of different branches and their aggregation into Block Credit Plan.
2. To review the progress in implementation of Block Credit Plan and the performance of each branch, in relation to its branch credit plan.
3. To consider the operational problems in the implementation of credit plans, with special reference to enlisting the co-operation of State Governments etc in provision of inputs, infrastructure and linkages.
4. To review the progress in the implementation of government sponsored programmes like, SGSY, SJSRY, PMRY, SLRS etc,. including their impact on the beneficiaries.
5. To allocate service areas to new branches opened in the block.
6. To monitor the recovery programmes and the adequacy of the steps taken in this regard, including the support available from the State Government machinery.

4

# Trend and Growth of Lead Bank Schemes

## INTRODUCTION

In this chapter, an attempt is made to analyse the financial assistance provided by commercial banks, under Lead Bank Scheme in Kanyakumari district.

Under the Lead Bank scheme, commercial banks are assigned one or more districts to co-ordinate the activities of banks and other developmental agencies in the district. One of the objectives of the Lead Bank Scheme is to generate employment, through Government sponsored programmes. The Government of India had initiated IRDP and DWCRA for reaching the poor with credit facilities. Later, the Government launched a few other programmes like PMRY, SGSY, SJSRY and TAHDCO to ameliorate the lot of the poor, through self-employment activities.

## FRAMEWORK OF ANALYSIS

In order to examine the growth of the number of branches, deposits, advances and lending and its stability over a period of ten years from 1999-2000 to 2008-09, the arithmetic mean ($\overline{X}$) and co-efficient of variation (C.V) of the following formula is used.

$$\text{Co-efficient of Variation (\%)} = \frac{S.D.}{\overline{X}} \times 100 \qquad \ldots(4.1)$$

Where

$S.D =$ Standard deviation

$\overline{X}$ = Mean

The trend and compound growth rates are computed for number of branches and deposits advanced, by adopting the semi-log trend model as given below:

$$\text{Log } Y = a + bt \qquad \ldots(4.2)$$

where

$Y$ = variable

$t$ = Time variable

and a and b are the parameters to be estimated.

The above model (4.2) was estimated by the method of least squares. The compound growth rate was calculated by using the following formula:

$$\text{Compound Growth Rate (\%)} = [\text{Anti log } b - 1] \times 100 \qquad \ldots(4.3)$$

## ADVANCES TO GOVERNMENT-SPONSORED SCHEMES BY COMMERCIAL BANKS UNDER LEAD BANK IN KANYAKUMARI DISTRICT

An attempt is made in this section, to analyse the advances of government-sponsored schemes, outstanding loans and recovery performance in commercial banks under Lead Bank Scheme in Kanyakumari district. For the analysis, the time series data form 1999-2000 to 2008-09 are taken into account.

### Number of Branches, Deposits and Advances in Commercial Banks in Kanyakumari District

The details about the number of branches, deposits and advances in commercial banks under Lead Bank Scheme in Kanyakumari district are shown in Table 4.1.

**Table 4.1: Number of Branches, Deposits, Advances in Commercial Banks in Kanyakumari District**

(*Rs in Lakhs*)

| Sl. No. | Year | Number of Branches | Percentage of Increase Over the Previous Year | Deposit Amount | Percentage of Increase Over the Previous Year | Advances Amount | Percentage of Increase Over the Previous Year |
|---|---|---|---|---|---|---|---|
| 1. | 1999-2000 | 147 | – | 125352 | – | 59917 | – |
| 2. | 2000-2001 | 147 | – | 143078 | 14.14 | 69503 | 16.00 |
| 3. | 2001-2002 | 147 | – | 167894 | 17.34 | 80172 | 15.35 |
| 4. | 2002-2003 | 151 | 2.72 | 187300 | 11.56 | 94330 | 17.65 |
| 5. | 2003-2004 | 152 | 0.66 | 207631 | 10.85 | 120420 | 27.65 |
| 6. | 2004-2005 | 156 | 2.63 | 223251 | 7.52 | 180023 | 49.49 |
| 7. | 2005-2006 | 158 | 1.28 | 249684 | 11.69 | 192682 | 7.03 |
| 8. | 2006-2007 | 169 | 6.96 | 286222 | 11.63 | 228359 | 18.52 |
| 9. | 2007-2008 | 171 | 1.18 | 319650 | 11.67 | 273992 | 19.98 |
| 10. | 2008-2009 | 176 | 2.92 | 445303 | 39.31 | 383366 | 39.92 |

*Source:* Compiled from the Annual Credit plan of IOB, Kanyakumari District, (Lead Bank) from 1999-2000 to 2008-2009.

From Table 4.1, it is observed that there is no remarkable increase in the number of branches in Kanyakumari district during the period under the study, and it has just increased from 147 branches in 1999-2000 to 176 branches in 2008-09. Regarding the deposits, a steady increase was found during the period under study. But a fluctuation was observed in the percentage of increase per annum. In the case of advances, it has steadily increased from Rs. 59,917 lakhs in the year 1999-2000 to Rs. 3,83,366 lakhs in 2008-09. The percentage of increase over the previous year showed certain fluctuations during the period under the study.

The average and stability of number of branches, deposits and advances to government-sponsored schemes by commercial banks in Kanyakumari district are shown in Table 4.2 below:

**Table 4.2: Average and Stability of Number of Branches, Deposits and Advances during the Period from 1999-2000 to 2008-09**

***(Rs. in Lakhs)***

| Sl. No. | Particulars | No. of Branches | Deposits | Advances |
|---|---|---|---|---|
| 1. | Mean | 157.40 | 235536.50 | 168276.40 |
| 2. | S.D | 10.86 | 95665.71 | 104775.68 |
| 3. | C.V (%) | 6.90 | 40.62 | 62.26 |

*Source:* Computed data.

It is observed from Table 4.2 that the average number of branches, deposits and advances made by commercial banks in Kanyakumari district was 157.40, Rs. 2,35,536.50 lakhs and Rs. 1,68,276.40 lakhs respectively during the period from 1999-2000 to 2008-09. It is observed from the analysis that high fluctuation was found in advances compared to deposits, as indicated by the co-efficient of variation.

The computed results of trend and growth rate of number of branches, the deposits and advances made by commercial banks under Lead Bank in Kanyakumari district are given in Table 4.3.

**Table 4.3: Trend and Growth in the Number of Branches, Deposits and Advances**

| Sl. No. | Particulars | Trend Co-efficient | | | CGR (%) |
|---|---|---|---|---|---|
| | | a | b | $R^2$ | |
| 1. | Number of Branches | 5.46 | 0.006* (10.857) | 0.92 | 0.69 |
| 2. | Deposits | 11.83 | 0.086* (12.96) | 0.95 | 9.06 |
| 3. | Advances | 10.76 | 0.124* (15.498) | 0.96 | 13.25 |

*Source:* Computed data. (Figures in the parentheses are t-value).

*Note:* *Indicates that the trend co-efficient are statistically significant at 5 per cent level.

It is inferred from Table 4.3 that the trend co-efficient for the number of branches, deposits and advances is statistically significant at 5 per cent level. It implies that on an average the number of branches and deposits have been increasing at the rate of 0.006 per cent and 0.086 per cent per annum respectively. The growth was found high in advances (13.25%) followed by deposits (9.06%) and number of branches (0.69%).

## Share of Commercial Banks' Lending to Government-sponsored Schemes in All Sectors

The following Table 4.4 shows the details about the share of commercial banks' lending to government-sponsored schemes in all sectors during the period from 1999-2000 to 2008-09.

It is inferred from Table 4.4 that the share of commercial banks' lending to Government-sponsored schemes in all sectors has not increased except during 2001-02. It is revealed that the maximum share was found in 2001-02. The commercial banks' lending to government-sponsored schemes ranged from Rs. 5,427 lakhs in 1999-2000 to Rs. 8,672 lakhs in 2008-09. Commercial Banks' lending to all sectors, ranged between Rs. 57,676 lakhs in 1999-2000 to Rs. 1,51,076 lakhs in

2008-09. From 2002-03 to 2008-09, the share of Government sponsored scheme in all sectors has been showing a downward trend.

**Table 4.4: Share of Commercial Banks' Lending to Government-sponsored Schemes in All Sectors in Kanyakumari District**

**(*Rs in Lakhs*)**

| Sl. No. | Year | Commercial Banks' Lending to All Sectors | Commercial Banks' Lending to Government Sponsored Schemes | Share of Commercial Banks' Lending to Government-Sponsored Scheme in all Sectors |
|---|---|---|---|---|
| 1. | 1999-2000 | 57676 | 5427 | 9.41 |
| 2. | 2000-2001 | 59782 | 5736 | 9.59 |
| 3. | 2001-2002 | 61934 | 6376 | 10.29 |
| 4. | 2002-2003 | 71996 | 6712 | 9.32 |
| 5. | 2003-2004 | 92316 | 6816 | 7.38 |
| 6. | 2004-2005 | 101355 | 6912 | 6.81 |
| 7. | 2005-2006 | 123634 | 7682 | 6.21 |
| 8. | 2006-2007 | 134722 | 8148 | 6.04 |
| 9. | 2007-2008 | 146137 | 8433 | 5.77 |
| 10. | 2008-2009 | 151076 | 8672 | 5.74 |

*Source:* Compiled from the Annual Credit plan of IOB, Kanyakumari District, (Lead Bank) from 1999-2000 to 2008-2009.

Table 4.5 shows the share of commercial banks' lending under Lead Bank to Government-sponsored schemes in priority sector advances.

From Table 4.5, it is understood that the priority sector advances by commercial banks showed an increasing trend from Rs. 39,376 lakhs in 1999-2000 to Rs. 72,448 lakhs in 2008-09. The share of government-sponsored scheme advances in priority sector, advances made by commercial banks in Kanyakumari district, had the highest percentage of 14.28 during 2001-02 and the lowest of 10.32 per cent during

2003-04. A fluctuating trend in the share of government sponsored scheme advances in priority sector advances was observed during the period of study.

**Table 4.5: Share of Commercial Banks' Lending to Government-sponsored Schemes in Priority Sector Advances in Kanyakumari District**

(*Rs. in Lakhs*)

| Sl. No. | Year | Priority Sector Advances | Government Sponsored Scheme Advances | Share of Government Sponsored Schemes Advances in Priority Sector Advances |
|---|---|---|---|---|
| 1. | 1999-2000 | 39376 | 5427 | 13.78 |
| 2. | 2000-2001 | 41249 | 5736 | 13.90 |
| 3. | 2001-2002 | 44559 | 6367 | 14.28 |
| 4. | 2002-2003 | 47260 | 6712 | 14.20 |
| 5. | 2003-2004 | 66047 | 6816 | 10.32 |
| 6. | 2004-2005 | 59381 | 6912 | 11.64 |
| 7. | 2005-2006 | 65546 | 7682 | 11.72 |
| 8. | 2006-2007 | 68184 | 8148 | 11.95 |
| 9. | 2007-2008 | 70216 | 8433 | 12.01 |
| 10. | 2008-2009 | 72448 | 8672 | 11.97 |

*Source:* Compiled from the Annual Credit plan of IOB, Kanyakumari District, (Lead Bank) from 1999-2000 to 2008-2009.

Table 4.6 indicates the average and stability of advances to all sectors, government-sponsored schemes and priority sector by commercial banks under Lead Bank, over the period from 1999-2000 to 2008-09.

It can be inferred from Table 4.6, that the average commercial lending to all sectors, government-sponsored scheme and priority sector were Rs. 1,00,062.80 lakhs, Rs. 7,091.40 lakhs and Rs. 57,426.60 lakhs respectively during the period from 1999-2000 to 2008-09. It is inferred from the analysis that a small fluctuation was found in government-sponsored scheme advances by commercial banks compared to commercial banks' lending to all sectors as indicated by the co-efficient of variation.

**Table 4.6: Average and Stability of Advances to All Sectors, Priority Sector and Government-sponsored Schemes by Commercial Banks during the Period from 1999-2000 to 2008-09**

***(Rs. in Lakhs)***

| Sl. No. | Particulars | Commercial Banks' Lending to All Sectors | Government Sponsored Schemes Advances by Commercial Banks | Priority Sector Advances by Commercial Banks |
|---|---|---|---|---|
| 1. | Mean | 100062.80 | 7091.40 | 57426.60 |
| 2. | S.D. | 36824.59 | 1112.28 | 12933.43 |
| 3. | C.V(%) | 36.80 | 15.68 | 22.52 |

*Source:* Computed data.

The following Table 4.7 shows, the computed results of trend and growth rates of advances to all sectors, advances to government-sponsored schemes and priority sector advances by commercial banks under Lead Bank in Kanyakumari district.

It is evident from Table 4.7 that the trend co-efficients of advances to all sectors and priority sector advances by commercial banks are statistically significant at 5 per cent level, whereas that of advances to government-sponsored schemes by commercial banks is not statistically significant at 5 per cent level. It implies that advances to all sectors, priority sector and to Government-sponsored schemes by commercial banks under Lead Bank schemes have been increasing at the rate of 0.1243 per cent, 0.074 per cent and 0.025 per cent per annum respectively. The growth was found high in advances to all sectors by commercial banks (13.25%) followed by priority sector advances (7.68%) and advances to government-sponsored schemes (2.56%) respectively.

**Table 4.7: Trend and Growth of Advances to All Sectors, Advances to Government-sponsored Schemes and Priority Sector Advances by Commercial Banks**

| Sl. No. | Particulars | Trend Co-efficient | | | CGR (%) |
|---|---|---|---|---|---|
| | | a | b | $\overline{R}^2$ | |
| 1. | Advances to all sectors by Commercial Banks | 10.76 | 0.1243* (15.498) | 0.96 | 13.25 |
| 2. | Advances to government sponsored schemes by Commercial Banks | 10.37 | 0.025 (1.774) | 0.19 | 2.56 |
| 3. | Priority sector advances by Commercial Banks | 10.52 | 0.074* (7.88) | 0.87 | 7.68 |

*Source:* Computed data. (Figures in the parentheses are *t* - values)

*Note:* *Indicates that the trend co- efficients are statistically significant at 5 per cent level.

## Actual Advances to Government Sponsored Schemes

The actual advances to government-sponsored schemes against commitment made by commercial banks during the period from 1999-2000 to 2008-09 are shown in the Table 4.8 below:

**Table 4.8: Actual Advances to Government-sponsored Schemes Against Commitment Made by Commercial Banks in Kanyakumari District**

**(*Rs in Lakhs*)**

| Sl. No. | Year | Target of Government Sponsored Schemes Advances Made by Commercial Banks | Percentage Increase Over the Previous Year | Actual Amount of Advances Made by Commercial Banks | Percentage of Increase Over the Previous Year |
|---|---|---|---|---|---|
| (1) | (2) | (3) | (4) | (5) | (6) |
| 1. | 1999-2000 | 6482 | – | 5427 | – |
| 2. | 2000-01 | 6716 | 3.61 | 5736 | 5.69 |
| 3. | 2001-02 | 7648 | 13.88 | 6367 | 10.48 |

*(Contd...)*

| (1) | (2) | (3) | (4) | (5) | (6) |
|---|---|---|---|---|---|
| 4. | 2002-03 | 7982 | 4.37 | 6712 | 5.42 |
| 5. | 2003-04 | 8578 | 7.47 | 6816 | 1.55 |
| 6. | 2004-05 | 8672 | 1.09 | 6912 | 1.41 |
| 7. | 2005-06 | 9018 | 3.98 | 7682 | 11.14 |
| 8. | 2006-07 | 9748 | 8.09 | 8148 | 6.07 |
| 9. | 2007-08 | 10546 | 8.19 | 8433 | 3.50 |
| 10. | 2008-09 | 11072 | 4.99 | 8672 | 2.83 |

*Source:* Compiled from the Annual Credit plan of IOB, Kanyakumari District, (Lead Bank) from 1999-2000 to 2008-2009.

From Table 4.8, it could be inferred that the commercial banks under Lead Bank Schemes have given less advances to government sponsored schemes than the targeted amount in almost all years of the study. The targeted amount ranged from Rs. 6,482 lakhs in 1999-2000 to Rs. 11,072 lakhs in 2008-09, while the actual advances ranged from Rs. 5,427 lakhs in the year 1999-2000 to Rs. 8,672 lakhs in 2008-09.

The average and stability of target amount of advances and actual advances to government-sponsored schemes by commercial banks in Kanyakumari district are given in Table 4.9.

**Table 4.9: Average and Stability of Target of Government-sponsored Schemes Advances by Commercial Banks Under Lead Bank and Actual Advances During the Period from 1999-2000 to 2008-09**

***(Rs in Lakhs)***

| Sl. No. | Particulars | Target of Government Sponsored Scheme Advances by Commercial Banks | Actual Advances |
|---|---|---|---|
| 1. | Mean | 8646.20 | 7090.50 |
| 2. | S.D | 1516.51 | 1112.93 |
| 3. | C.V (%) | 17.54 | 15.70 |

*Source:* Computed data.

It is possible to infer from Table 4.9 that the average target of Government sponsored scheme advances made by commercial banks under Lead Bank Schemes and the actual advances made by them in Kanyakumari district were Rs. 8,646.20 lakhs and Rs. 7,090.50 lakhs respectively during the period from 1999-2000 to 2008-09. It is also inferred from the analysis that a high fluctuation was found in the target of government-sponsored scheme advances made by commercial banks compared to the actual advances as indicated by the co-efficient of variation.

The computed results in trend and growth rates of the target of government-sponsored scheme advances by commercial banks and actual advances in Kanyakumari district are given in Table 4.10.

**Table 4.10: Trend and Growth of Target of Government-sponsored Schemes Advances by Commercial Banks Under Lead Bank and Actual Advances**

| Sl. No. | Particulars | Trend Co-efficient | | | CGR (%) |
|---|---|---|---|---|---|
| | | a | b | $\overline{R}^2$ | |
| 1. | Target of Government sponsored scheme advances made by Commercial Banks | 8.73 | 0.058* (19.65) | 0.98 | 5.97 |
| 2. | Actual advances | 8.56 | 0.052* (17.46) | 0.97 | 5.33 |

*Source:* Computed data. (Figures in the brackets are *t* - values)

Note: *Indicates that the trend co-efficients are statistically significant at 5 per cent level.

It is obvious from the Table 4.10 that the trend co-efficients of the target of government-sponsored scheme advances by commercial banks under Lead Bank Schemes and actual advances are statistically significant at 5 per cent level and positive. It implies that on an average, the target of government-sponsored scheme advances by commercial banks under Lead Bank Schemes and the actual advances have been increasing at the rate of 0.058 per cent and 0.052 per cent per annum respectively. The growth was found high in the target of government-sponsored scheme advances by commercial banks (5.97%) during the period of the study followed by actual advances (5.33%) in Kanyakumari district.

## Outstanding Advances to Priority Sector and Government-sponsored Schemes by Commercial Banks Under Lead Bank Schemes

Table 4.11 (*See on next page*) presents the outstanding advances to priority sector and government-sponsored schemes by commercial banks under Lead Bank Schemes during the period from 1999-2000 to 2008-09.

From Table 4.11, it is found that the total outstanding advances to commercial banks increased from Rs. 17,733 lakhs in 2000-01 to Rs. 28,423 lakhs in 2008-09. The outstanding advances estimated in priority sector increased from Rs. 7,231 lakhs in 1999-2000 to Rs. 12,167 lakhs in 2008-09. A small fluctuation was observed in the total outstanding advances over the period, compared to that in the priority sector. The priority sector outstanding increased from 32.91 per cent in 1999-2000 to 42.28 per cent in 2000-01. The outstanding in Government-sponsored schemes increased from Rs. 3,693 lakhs in 1999-2000 to Rs. 5,167 lakhs in 2008-09. The total outstanding in government sponsored schemes was the highest during 2000-01 and it was the lowest during 2005-06, the percentage being 21.27 and 15.58 respectively.

The average and stability of outstanding in total advances, priority sector advances and Government-sponsored scheme advances over the period of study are given in Table 4.12. (*See on page 103*)

Table 4.12 reveals that the average outstanding in total advances, priority sector advances and government-sponsored scheme advances by commercial banks were Rs. 24,431.10 lakhs, Rs. 9,977.80 lakhs and Rs. 4164.20 lakhs respectively during the period 1999-2000 to 2008-09. It is also inferred that a high fluctuation was found in priority sector compared to government-sponsored scheme credit as indicated by the co-efficient of variation.

**Table 4.11: Outstanding Advances to Priority Sector and Government-sponsored Schemes by Commercial Banks in Kanyakumari District**

(*Rs. in Lakhs*)

| Sl. No. | Year | Total Outstanding Advances | Outstanding Advances to Priority Sector | Percentage of Priority Sector to Total Advances | Outstanding Advances to Government Sponsored Scheme | Percentage of Government Sponsored Scheme Advances to Total Advances |
|---|---|---|---|---|---|---|
| 1. | 1999-2000 | 21970 | 7231 | 32.91 | 3693 | 16.81 |
| 2. | 2000-2001 | 17733 | 7498 | 42.28 | 3772 | 21.27 |
| 3. | 2001-2002 | 21116 | 7462 | 35.34 | 3842 | 18.19 |
| 4. | 2002-2003 | 23921 | 8524 | 35.63 | 3901 | 16.31 |
| 5. | 2003-2004 | 24862 | 10218 | 41.10 | 4284 | 17.23 |
| 6. | 2004-2005 | 24973 | 11673 | 46.74 | 4087 | 16.37 |
| 7. | 2005-2006 | 26321 | 11562 | 43.93 | 4101 | 15.58 |
| 8. | 2006-2007 | 27521 | 11376 | 41.34 | 4421 | 16.06 |
| 9. | 2007-2008 | 27471 | 12067 | 43.93 | 4374 | 15.92 |
| 10. | 2008-2009 | 28423 | 12167 | 42.28 | 5167 | 18.18 |

*Source:* Compiled from the Annual Credit plan of IOB, Kanyakumari District, (Lead Bank) from 1999-2000 to 2008-2009.

**Table 4.12: Average and Stability of Outstanding in Total Advances, Priority Sector Advances and Government Sponsored Scheme Advances during the Period from 1999-2000 to 2008-09**

**(*Rs. in Lakhs*)**

| Sl. No. | Particulars | Total Advances | Priority Sector Advances | Government Sponsored Scheme Advances |
|---|---|---|---|---|
| 1. | Mean | 24431.10 | 9977.80 | 4164.20 |
| 2. | S.D | 3349.07 | 2073.39 | 433.18 |
| 3. | C.V (%) | 13.71 | 20.78 | 10.40 |

*Source:* Computed data.

The computed results of trend and growth rates in outstanding for total advances; priority sector advances and government-sponsored scheme advances by commercial banks in Kanyakumari are given in Table 4.13.

**Table 4.13: Trend and Growth of Outstanding in Total Advances, Priority Sector Advances and Government Sponsored Scheme Advances**

| Sl. No. | Particulars | Trend Co-efficient | | | CGR (%) |
|---|---|---|---|---|---|
| | | a | b | $\overline{R}^2$ | |
| 1. | Total advances | 9.86 | 0.042* (5.22) | 0.74 | 4.33 |
| 2. | Priority sector advances | 8.81 | 0.068* (7.65) | 0.86 | 7.00 |
| 3. | Government sponsored scheme advances | 8.17 | 0.029* (5.81) | 0.78 | 2.99 |

*Source:* Computed data. (Figures in the parentheses are *t* - values)

*Note:* *Indicates that the trend co-efficients are statistically significant at 5 per cent level.

It is evident from Table 4.13 that the trend co-efficient of outstanding in total advances, priority sector advances and government-sponsored scheme advances are statistically significant at 5 per cent level and positive. It implies that on an average, outstanding in total advances, priority sector advances and government-sponsored scheme advances have been increasing at the rate of 0.042 per cent, 0.068 per cent and 0.029 per cent per annum respectively. The growth was found high in priority sector (7.00%) followed by total advances (4.33%) and in the Government-sponsored scheme advances, it was 2.99 per cent in Kanyakumari district.

### Recovery Position of Commercial Banks in Kanyakumari District

Table 4.14 shows the details about the demand, collection, overdue and percentage of recovery in commercial banks in Kanyakumari district.

**Table 4.14: Percentage of Recovery Position of Commercial Banks in Kanyakumari District**

**(*Rs in Lakhs*)**

| Sl. No. | Year | Demand | Collection | Overdue | Recovery Percentage |
|---|---|---|---|---|---|
| 1. | 1999-2000 | 16943 | 12200 | 4743 | 72 |
| 2. | 2000-2001 | 19353 | 12361 | 6992 | 64 |
| 3. | 2001-2002 | 24183 | 17494 | 6689 | 72 |
| 4. | 2002-2003 | 24224 | 16472 | 7752 | 68 |
| 5. | 2003-2004 | 25661 | 18436 | 7225 | 72 |
| 6. | 2004-2005 | 25674 | 17972 | 7702 | 70 |
| 7. | 2005-2006 | 19556 | 16427 | 3129 | 84 |
| 8. | 2006-2007 | 20321 | 17476 | 2845 | 86 |
| 9. | 2007-2008 | 21140 | 18392 | 2748 | 87 |
| 10. | 2008-2009 | 21683 | 18647 | 3036 | 86 |

*Source:* Compiled from the Annual Credit plan of IOB, Kanyakumari District, (Lead Bank) from 1999-2000 to 2008-2009.

From Table 4.14, it is found that the demand has ranged from Rs. 16,943 lakhs in 1999-2000 to Rs. 25,674 lakhs in 2004-05, whereas in the collection it ranged from Rs. 12,200 lakhs in 1999-2000 to Rs. 18,647 lakhs in 2008-09. The overdue in the commercial banks ranged from Rs. 4,743 lakhs in 1999-2000 to Rs. 7,752 lakhs in 2002-03. It is inferred that there was a fluctuation in overdue during the period under study. The rate of recovery ranged from 64 per cent in 2000-01 to 87 per cent in 2007-08. The rate of recovery is more than 70 per cent in eight out of the ten years of study.

Table 4.15 shows the average and stability in demand, collection and overdue over the period.

**Table 4.15: Average and Stability of Demand, Collection and Overdue in Commercial Banks in Kanyakumari District During the Period from 1999-2000 to 2008-09**

*(Rs. in Lakhs)*

| Sl. No. | Particulars | Demand | Collection | Overdue |
|---|---|---|---|---|
| 1. | Mean | 21873.80 | 16587.70 | 5286.10 |
| 2. | S.D | 2956.46 | 2394.33 | 2184.97 |
| 3. | C.V (%) | 13.52 | 14.43 | 41.33 |

*Source:* Computed data.

Table 4.15 shows that the averages of demand, collection and overdue of commercial banks in Kanyakumari district were Rs. 21,873.80 lakhs, Rs. 16,587.70 lakhs and Rs. 5,286.10 lakhs respectively during the period from 1999-2000 to 2008-09. It is inferred from the analysis that high fluctuation was found in overdue, compared to the collection as indicated by the co- efficient of variation.

The computed results of trend and growth rate of demand, collection and overdue in commercial banks under Lead Bank Schemes in Kanyakumari district are given in Table 4.16.

From Table 4.16, it could be inferred that the trend co-efficient of collection is statistically significant at 5 per cent level and positive whereas overdue is statistically significant at 5 per cent and negative. It implies that collection has been increasing at the rate of 0.04 per cent per annum while overdue has been decreasing at the rate of 0.11 per cent per annum. The growth was found high in collection (4.06%) followed by demand (0.80%) and negative growth is found in overdue (-10.05%).

**Table 4.16: Trend and Growth of Demand, Collection and Overdue in Commercial Banks Under Lead Bank Schemes in Kanyakumari District**

| Sl. No. | Particulars | Trend Co-efficient | | | CGR (%) |
|---|---|---|---|---|---|
| | | a | b | $\overline{R}^2$ | |
| 1. | Demand | 9.94 | 0.008 (0.51) | - 0.09 | 0.80 |
| 2. | Collection | 9.49 | 0.04* (3.28) | 0.52 | 4.06 |
| 3. | Overdue | 9.07 | - 0.11* (- 2.83) | 0.44 | - 10.05 |

*Source:* Computed data. (Figures in parentheses indicate *t* - values)

*Note:* *Indicates that the trend co-efficients are statistically significant at 5 per cent level.

5

# Evaluation of Lead Bank Schemes

## *Block-wise Comparison of Growth and Equity*

### INTRODUCTION

The basic objective of lead bank lendings through commercial banks to the government-sponsored programmes such as SJSRY, SGSY, PMRY and TAHDCO, is to generate employment opportunities for the people. In this chapter, an attempt is made to measure and compare the fund allocated for each government-sponsored programme from growth and equity angles in different blocks of Kanyakumari district. The fund allocated for the implementation of the programme, amongst the blocks, has been examined on the basis of the government-sponsored programmes, namely: *(i)* SJSRY; *(ii)* SGSY; *(iii)* PMRY; and *(iv)* TAHDCO. For this, the funds allocated for each scheme by Lead Bank in Kanyakumari district, for a period of 5 years from 2004-05 to 2008-09, have been taken up for analysis.

### THE ANALYTICAL FRAMEWORK

In order to examine the growth of the fund allocated by Lead Bank for various government-sponsored programmes, the compound growth rates are used. Further, to identify the performance variation and equity in the amount of loan sanctioned for this government-sponsored programmes amongst the blocks, in the district, for the years 2004-05 to 2008-09, the taxonomic method is used. This method has been used to construct the performance index. The measure of performance under this method is always non-negative. It lies between 0 and 1. The closer the measure of performance is to 0, the highest is the level of performance of the centres in the scheme. On the other hand, the measure closer to '1' indicates lower level of performance. In addition to facilitating the ranking of centres by the level of performance, the pattern and measure of development are useful in identifying the regions which serve as 'models' and in fixing the potential target of each indicator, for a given centre. The important step in the taxonomic method is to find out the difference or distance from each block to every other block for each of the standardized value of the selected indicators. The values, thus obtained, are arranged in the matrix form. It is named as the distance matrix. It is highly useful for fixing the potential targets, required for each of the schemes for the blocks. If the distance between any block and every other block is longer than the critical minimum distance (CMD) and shorter than the critical value (CV), the blocks would not join any sub-group and is called a typical centre. It may also be noted that a typical block need not necessarily be far less developed or far more developed than others, although a far more or far less developed block is a typical one[1].

The various steps involved in the taxonomic method are as follows:

### Step 1: Schemes and blocks

Selection of schemes and blocks has been made first and the original data on fund allocated for each scheme is to be arranged in a matrix $A_{nm}$ ($n$-blocks and $m$-schemes).

---

1 Namasivayam, D., "NREP in Tamil Nadu: Comparison of Growth and Equality by Taxonomic Method", *Margin*, October-December 1987, p. 58.

## Step 2: Standardization of variables

As the value of indicators may be in different units, standardization of the variable is to be done by using the following formula:

$$S_{ij} = \frac{X_{ij} - \overline{X}_i}{S_i}$$

where

$S_{ij}$ = Standardised value of *i*th scheme of *j*th block

$x_{ij}$ = Original value of *i*th scheme of *j*th block

$\overline{x}_i$ = Mean value of ith scheme, and

$S_i$ = Standard Deviation of *i*th scheme.

$s_{nm}$ denotes the standardised matrix.

## Step 3: Computation of pattern

From the standardized matrix $s_{nm}$, an ideal for each scheme (having maximum/minimum standardized value, depending upon the direction of the scheme) is identified and from this, deviation of the value for each block is taken for the schemes using the following formula.

$$P_i = \sqrt{\sum_{k=l}^{m} (S_{ik} - S_{ok})^2}$$

where,

$P_i$ denotes the pattern of development for the *i*th block.

$S_{ik}$ is the standardized value for the *i*th block and *k*th scheme, and

$S_{ok}$ is the best standardized value for the *k*th scheme.

For example, for the second block, the pattern value would be

$$P_i = \sqrt{(S_{21} - S_{01})^2 + (S_{22} - S_{02})^2 \ldots\ldots + (S_{2m} - S_{om})^2}$$

## Step 4: Computation of 'measure'

The 'measure' is denoted by $M_i$ and is obtained through the following formula:

$$M_i = \frac{P_i}{P}$$

where,

$P_i$ is the pattern value of the ith block and $P = \overline{P} + 2\,P_s$ and

$$\overline{P} = \frac{\sum_{i=1}^{n} P_i}{n} \text{ and}$$

$$\overline{P}_s = \sqrt{\frac{\sum^{n} (P_i - \overline{P})^2}{n}}$$

**Step 5: Fixing of initial targets**

Initial target can be fixed for each block, on each scheme, using the distance matrix, which is obtained by the following formula:

***(i)* Distance matrix**

$$D_{ab} = \sqrt{\sum_{k=1}^{m} (S_{ak} - S_{bk})^2}$$

where

$D_{ab}$ is an element in the distance matrix and

$a = 1, 2 \ldots n, b = 1, 2 \ldots n.$

The value of diagonal elements in the distance matrix is zero. For example, $D_{12}$ $(a=1, b=2)$ would be

$$\sqrt{(S_{11} - S_{21})^2 + (S_{12} - S_{22})^2 \ldots. + (S_{1m} - S_{2m})^2}$$

The distance matrix takes the form minimum value *dj*

$$\begin{pmatrix} 0 & d_{12} & d_{13} & \dots & d_{1n} \\ d_{21} & 0 & d_{23} & \dots & d_{2n} \\ . & . & . & \dots & . \\ . & . & . & \dots & . \\ d_{n1} & d_{n2} & d_{n3} & \dots & 0 \end{pmatrix} \begin{matrix} d_1 \\ d_2 \\ . \\ . \\ d_n \end{matrix}$$

**(ii) Critical Minimum Distance (CMD) and Critical Value (CV)**

For computing the critical minimum distance and critical value, the following formulae are used:

$CMD = \bar{d} + 2\ SD\ (dj)$

$CV \quad = \bar{d} - 2\ SD\ (dj)$

where

$$\bar{d} = \frac{\sum_{j=1}^{n}}{n} \text{ and } SD\ (d_j) = \sqrt{\frac{\sum_{j=1}^{n} (d_j - \bar{d})^2}{n}}$$

**(iii) Fixing targets**

For example, for block 'A', the model blocks are to be identified. These are those centres with the following conditions:

1. Their measures of development of performance are higher than that of 'A' and
2. The individual distance between 'A' and these blocks should not exceed CMD.

It must be noted that these serve as model blocks for a given block on all the indicators. After the identifications of model blocks, the arithmetic mean of the original value of the indicator has to be computed. This value is referred to as the potential target for block 'A' for a given scheme, which will be compared with the actual value for block 'A' on that indicator. Sometimes, it may happen that the potential target is less than the actual value for the block on the indicator. The procedure is to be repeated for a given block for all schemes chosen.

## ANALYSIS OF BLOCK-WISE PERFORMANCE

In this section, the centres' performance, with regard to the implementation of government sponsored programmes, in terms of allocation of funds, has been analysed under three heads namely *(i)* Growth Analysis; *(ii)* Classification Analysis; and *(iii)* Equity Analysis.

### Growth Analysis

Table 5.1 and 5.2 give the compound growth rates regarding the funds allocated, as the indicators on government sponsored programmes for the blocks in the district during the period 2004-05 to 2008-09.

**Table 5.1: Growth rate of Funds Allocated to Various Government Sponsored Programmes in Kanyakumari District During the Period from 2004-05 to 2008-09**

**(*Per Cent Per Annum*)**

| Sl. No. | Indicators | SJSRY | SGSY | PMRY | TAHDCO |
|---|---|---|---|---|---|
| 1. | Agasteeswaram | 6.23 | 7.14 | 4.20 | 3.91 |
| 2. | Killiyoor | 8.14 | 6.20 | 6.70 | 4.14 |
| 3. | Kurunthencode | 10.15 | 14.19 | 9.21 | 5.71 |
| 4. | Melpuram | 7.62 | 6.17 | 8.16 | 4.71 |
| 5. | Munchirai | 7.84 | 11.22 | 10.21 | 7.10 |
| 6. | Rajakkamangalam | 12.60 | 16.70 | 14.60 | 9.40 |
| 7. | Thiruvattar | 9.22 | 12.15 | 10.14 | 4.14 |
| 8. | Thovalai | 6.81 | 8.12 | 7.68 | 6.71 |
| 9. | Thuckalay | 6.91 | 9.21 | 8.21 | 5.40 |
| | **Overall** | **7.68** | **10.46** | **8.82** | **6.47** |

*Source:* Computed data.

**Table 5.2: Two Way Classification of Compound Growth Rates of Allocation of Funds to Various Government-Sponsored Programmes in Kanyakumari District**

| Sl. No | Indicators | Above Average | Below Average (Low) | Overall Growth Rate |
|---|---|---|---|---|
| 1. | SJSRY | Killiyoor<br>Kurunthencode<br>Munchirai<br>Rajakkamangalam<br>Thiruvattar | Agasteeswaram<br>Melpuram<br>Thovalai<br>Thuckalay | 7.68 |
| 2. | SGSY | Kurunthencode<br>Munchirai<br>Rajakkamangalam<br>Thiruvattar | Agasteeswaram<br>Melpuram<br>Thovalai<br>Thuckalay<br>Killiyoor | 10.46 |
| 3. | PMRY | Kurunthencode<br>Munchirai<br>Rajakkamangalam<br>Thiruvattar | Agasteeswaram<br>Killiyoor<br>Melpuram<br>Thovalai<br>Thuckalay | 8.82 |
| 4. | TAHDCO | Munchirai<br>Rajakkamangalam<br>Thovalai | Agasteeswaram<br>Killiyoor<br>Kurunthencode<br>Melpuram<br>Thiruvattar<br>Thuckalay | 6.47 |

*Source:* Computed data.

From Tables 5.1 and 5.2, it is observed that according to the growth rate of amount disbursed to SJSRY, the highest growth rate was found in Rajakkamangalam followed by Kurunthencode and Thiruvattar whereas the least growth rate was found in the following blocks namely Agasteeswaram, Thovalai and Thuckalay.

In the case of the growth rate of amount disbursed to SGSY, the highest growth rate was found in Rajakkamangalam and Kurunthencode whereas the blocks like Melpuram, Agasteeswaram and Thovalai showed lower growth rates.

Further, it also shows that in the case of growth rate of amount disbursed under PMRY, the highest growth rate was found in Rajakkamangalam while the lowest growth rate was found in Agasteeswaram.

It is also inferred that according to the growth rate of amount disbursed under TAHDCO, the blocks like Munchirai, Thovalai and Kurunthencode showed much better performance than the remaining blocks.

As to the performance of various blocks, the analysis underscores the fact that Kurunthencode, Rajakkanmangalam and Thiruvattar had registered higher overall growth rate in the allocation of funds under SJSRY Scheme. With regard to the SGSY scheme, Killiyoor and Rajakkamangalam have had high growth in the allocation of funds by Lead bank. The overall growth rate of the PMRY scheme was higher in Rajakkamangalam, Thiruvattar and Munchirai blocks. In the case of TAHDCO, Rajakkamangalam and Thovalai have registered higher overall growth rate in the allocation of funds by the Lead Bank in Kanyakumari district.

## Classification Analysis

On the basis of each of the four selected government-sponsored scheme programmes, the blocks could be identified, ranked and classified on the basis of the fund allocated and disbursed during a period of 5 years (2004-05 to 2008-09). Ranking of blocks in Kanyakumari district on the basis of government-sponsored programmes like SJSRY, SGSY, PMRY and TAHDCO is presented in Table 5.3.

From Table 5.3, it is inferred that the fund allocated to SJSRY scheme by Lead bank was found high in the blocks namely Rajakkamangalam, Killiyoor and Munchirai, whereas it was found low in the blocks namely Thovalai, Thuckalay and Agasteeswaram.

**Table 5.3: Ranking of Blocks in Kanyakumari District on the Basis of the Average Amount Allocated for Five Years Under Government-sponsored Programmme (2004-05 to 2008-09)**

| Sl. No. | Centres | SJSRY | SGSY | PMRY | TAHDCO |
|---|---|---|---|---|---|
| 1. | Agasteeswaram | 7 | 4 | 6 | 5 |
| 2. | Killiyoor | 2 | 3 | 2 | 2 |
| 3. | Kurunthencode | 5 | 5 | 3 | 6 |
| 4. | Melpuram | 6 | 6 | 7 | 7 |
| 5. | Munchirai | 3 | 2 | 4 | 4 |
| 6. | Rajakkamangalam | 1 | 1 | 1 | 1 |
| 7. | Thiruvattar | 4 | 7 | 5 | 3 |
| 8. | Thovalai | 9 | 9 | 9 | 9 |
| 9. | Thuckalay | 8 | 8 | 8 | 8 |

*Source:* Computed from actual value.

Rajakkamangalam, Munchirai, Killiyoor and Thiruvattar are the four blocks where the funds allocated to SGSY scheme by Lead bank is high. On the other hand in Thovalai, Thuckalay and Thiruvattar, the funds allocated to SGSY is relatively low.

In the case of funds allocated and disbursed under PMRY scheme by Lead bank, the blocks namely Rajakkamangalam, Killiyoor and Kurunthencode have shown better performance compared to other blocks.

Further, it is also found that the funds allocated to TAHDCO by Lead bank were found high in the blocks namely Rajakkamangalam, Killiyoor, and Kurunthencode whereas, it was found low in Thovalai, Thuckalay and Melpuram.

The values of the 'pattern' and 'measure' for each block on the basis of government-sponsored scheme programmes in the district during 2004-05 to 2008-09 are given in Table 5.4.

**Table 5.4: Pattern and Measure of Lead Bank Schemes Among the Blocks in Kanyakumari District during the Period from 2004-06 to 2008-09**

| Sl. No. | Centres | Pattern (Pi) | Measure (M1) | Rank |
|---|---|---|---|---|
| 1. | Rajakkamangalam | 1.2016 | 0.0918 | I |
| 2. | Killiyoor | 2.6672 | 0.2097 | II |
| 3. | Agasteeswaram | 3.6512 | 0.2781 | III |
| 4. | Melpuram | 5.4141 | 0.4031 | IV |
| 5. | Munchirai | 5.9412 | 0.4396 | V |
| 6. | Kurunthencode | 6.6649 | 0.5121 | VI |
| 7. | Thiruvattar | 7.4752 | 0.5681 | VII |
| 8. | Thovalai | 7.3578 | 0.5862 | VIII |
| 9. | Thuckalay | 7.7314 | 0.6012 | IX |

*Source:* Computed data.

It has been inferred from Table 5.4, that out of the 9 blocks, Rajakkamangalam, Killiyoor, Agasteeswarm and Melpuram ranked first, second, third and fourth while Thuckalay ranked the last on the basis of four selected government-sponsored programmes under Lead Bank schemes in Kanyakumari district. The remaining blocks fell in-between these rankings.

## Equity Analysis

This kind of analysis would help to find out the direction of inequity existing among the schemes, regarding the funds allocated under Lead Bank Schemes in each block of the district.

The potential target and actual values of the amount allocated for each of the schemes among the blocks are given in Table 5.5. The potential targets have been computed with the help of the distance matrix presented in Table 5.6. (*See on page 118*) Table 5.5 shows that the amount disbursed for the scheme SJSRY was found high for the block Rajakkamangalam. Hence, this block has been chosen as the

**Table 5.5: Estimate of Potential Targets and Actual Value of Funds Allocated for Each Block on Various Lead Bank Schemes**

(*Rs. in Lakhs*)

| Sl. No. | Indicators | SJSRY | SGSY | PMRY | TAHDCO |
|---|---|---|---|---|---|
| 1. | Agasteeswaram | 564 (3241) | 7812* (7648) | 1982 (2943) | 586* (485) |
| 2. | Killiyoor | 2432 (3241) | 10689 (12467) | 5263 (5926) | 948 (1152) |
| 3. | Kurunthencode | 1240 (3241) | 7648 (12467) | 2943* (5926) | 485 (1142) |
| 4. | Melpuram | 862 (2380) | 7241 (10235) | 1064 (5323) | 242 (824) |
| 5. | Munchirai | 1849 (2379) | 8849 (8355) | 3121 (4302) | 642 (907) |
| 6. | Rajakkamangalam | 3241** | 12467** | 5926** | 1152** |
| 7. | Thiruvattar | 1752 (2166) | 6452 (10143) | 3111 (4593) | 742 (868) |
| 8. | Thovalai | 486 (1939) | 4041 (9139) | 321 (3685) | 49 (746) |
| 9. | Thuckalay | 501 (1476) | 4841 (6075) | 542 (2075) | 96 (475) |

*Source:* Computed data. (Figures in brackets indicates potential targets)

*Note:* *Actual values are higher than the potential targets.

**Model centre for other centres.

model block of the district. No other blocks have the actuals more than the potentials under SJSRY scheme. Further, it is inferred from the analysis that Rajakkamangalam block has shown equity in achievement, while the other centres have not shown equity in the achievement of funds allocated under Lead Bank schemes.

By comparing the actual value of funds allocated with the potential target of each block under SGSY scheme, it is observed that Rajakkamangalam block has shown equity in achievement and it is a model block in the district. Further, the fund allocated

**Table 5.6: Distance Matrix of Performance Across the Centres in Kanyakumari District**

| Sl. No. | Name of the Blocks | Centre Code | 1 | 2 | 3 | 4 | 5 | 6 | 7 | 8 | 9 |
|---|---|---|---|---|---|---|---|---|---|---|---|
| 1. | Agasteeswaram | (1) | – | | | | | | | | |
| 2. | Killiyoor | (2) | 5.2945 | – | | | | | | | |
| 3. | Kurunthencode | (3) | 3.0011 | 3.9915 | – | | | | | | |
| 4. | Melpuram | (4) | 3.6924 | 7.9911 | 5.5611 | – | | | | | |
| 5. | Munchirai | (5) | 4.5916 | 0.8911 | 3.2915 | 7.9115 | – | | | | |
| 6. | Rajakkamangalam | (6) | 5.2315 | 0.3911 | 3.4112 | 8.2315 | 0.8315 | – | | | |
| 7. | Thiruvattar | (7) | 5.7919 | 0.6115 | 4.4911 | 8.8516 | 1.3916 | 0.6511 | – | | |
| 8. | Thovalai | (8) | 5.5315 | 0.2615 | 4.2115 | 8.9115 | 0.9921 | 0.3711 | 0.3321 | – | |
| 9. | Thuckalay | (9) | 4.9316 | 0.8121 | 3.5411 | 8.2115 | 0.4921 | 0.4911 | 1.1151 | 0.8111 | – |

$\overline{d}$ = 1.1649 S.D. = 0.9259 CMD = 3.0167 CV = (–) 0.7948

was higher for this block under SGSY scheme. In Agasteeswaram block, the actual value is greater than the potential target. But this is not the case for other centres. Rajakkamangalam has received the highest fund allocation under SGSY schemes. Higher inequity in the disbursement of loan was observed in other blocks.

In the case of PMRY scheme, Rajakkamangalam has been chosen as the model block of the district. In Agasteeswaram, the actual value is greater than the potential value. The fund allocated under PMRY scheme in Rajakkamangalam block, has been found equity with the potential targets. All other blocks exhibit high inequity in the fund allocation under Lead Bank schemes for PMRY programme.

By comparing the actual fund allocation with the potential target of each block under TAHDCO, it is observed that Rajakkamangalam block has shown equity in amount disbursement, while the other blocks have not shown equity in fund allocation. Rajakkamangalam is the only model block for other blocks in the district. In Agasteesearam, the actual value is greater than the potential value.

Table 5.6 shows the distance matrix of performance across the centres in Kanyakumari district.

The distance matrix given in Table 5.6 shows always only one block with shortest distance to the corresponding taluks in each row. For example, Kurunthencode is the only centre at the shortest distance of 3.0011 to Agasteeswaram and again Thovalai at the shortest distance of 0.2615 to Kurunthencode in the second row.

## SUMMARY

The findings of the analysis are summarized below:

Regarding the growth analysis, the fund allocated under SJSRY scheme, was found to have the highest rate of growth in Rajakkamagalam followed by Killiyoor. In the case of SGSY and PMRY schemes, the highest growth rate of fund allocated was found in Rajakkamangalam block. Regarding the fund allocated under TAHDCO, the highest growth rate was observed in Rajakkamangalam block followed by Killiyoor.

According to the classification analysis, ranking of blocks in Kanyakumari district shows that Rajakkamangalam stands first in the fund allocation. Next to this, Killiyoor has benefited much under Lead Bank schemes. The values of patterns and measure show that Rajakkamangalam ranks first and Thuckalay last. The other seven blocks fall in between these two blocks. Rajakkamangalam is the only model block for all other blocks in Kanyakumari district.

Agasteeswaram block had the distinction of achieving more than the target in SGSY, PRMY and TAHDCO schemes. The equity analysis infers that there is inequity in the fund allocation in all four schemes among the blocks except Rajakkamangalam.

6

# Impact of Government Sponsored Programmes Under the Lead Bank Scheme on Income, Asset, Employment Generation and Recovery Performance

## INTRODUCTION

The Government-sponsored programmes under the Lead Bank Scheme specially aim at bringing the beneficiary families above the poverty line, by ensuring appreciable and sustained level of income over a period of time. An evaluation study is attempted to identify the problems connected with the implementation of the Lead Bank Scheme and analyse the prospects for development in future. 300 beneficiaries were interviewed through interview schedules to assess the income, asset, employment generation and recovery performance. This analytical chapter is divided into the following four sections:

1 Characteristics of sample beneficiaries;
2. Income, asset and employment generation;
3. Factors influencing the repayment of loan;
4. Recovery performance; and
5. The views of bankers and beneficiaries.

## Characteristics of Sample Beneficiaries

This section attempts to describe the characteristics of the sample beneficiaries.

Table 6.1 presents the distribution of the sample respondents according to their age.

**Table 6.1: Age-wise Classification of the Sample Beneficiaries**

| Sl. No. | Age (in years) | Non-Agricultural Activities | Agriculture and Allied Activities |
|---|---|---|---|
| 1. | Below 30 | 27 (26.47) | 19 (9.60) |
| 2. | 30-40 | 48 (47.06) | 95 (47.98) |
| 3. | 40-50 | 21 (20.59) | 68 (34.34) |
| 4. | 50 and above | 6 (5.88) | 16 (8.08) |
| | **Total** | **102 (100)** | **198 (100)** |

*Source:* Primary data (Figures in parentheses indicate the percentage)

Age-wise classification of the sample respondents is furnished in Table 6.1. It is observed that out of 102 beneficiaries engaged in non-agricultural activities, 27 (26.47%) fall in the age group of below 30 years, about 48 (47.06%) fall in the age group of 30-40 years, 21 (20.59%) and 6 (5.88%) of them in the age groups of 40-50 years and 50 years and above respectively.

Further, it has been also observed that out of 198 beneficiaries engaged in agricultural and allied activities, 19 (9.60%) fall in the age group of below 30 years, 95 (47.98%) fall in the age group of 30-40 years, 68 (34.34%) and 16 (8.08%) in the age group of 40-50 years and 50 years and above respectively.

Thus, it is concluded from the analysis that more than 45 per cent of the beneficiaries belong to the age group of 30-40 years, in both sectors in the study area.

Table 6.2 shows the sex of the sample respondents.

**Table 6.2: Sex of the Sample Beneficiaries**

| Sl. No. | Sex | Non-Agricultural Activities | Agriculture and Allied Activities |
|---|---|---|---|
| 1. | Male | 61 (59.80) | 122 (61.62) |
| 2. | Female | 41 (40.20) | 76 (38.38) |
| | **Total** | **102 (100)** | **198 (100)** |

*Source:* Primary data (Figures in parentheses indicate the percentage)

From Table 6.2, it is observed that in the case of non-agricultural activities, out of 102 respondents, 61 (59.80%) were male while the remaining 41 (40.20%) were female respondents. In the case of agriculture and allied activities, out of 198 sample respondents, 122 (61.62%) are male and the remaining 76 (38.38%) are female respectively.

Table 6.3 shows the educational status of the beneficiaries in non-agricultural and agricultural sectors.

**Table 6.3: Educational Qualification of the Sample Beneficiaries**

| Sl. No. | Category | Non-Agricultural Activities | Agriculture and Allied Activities |
|---|---|---|---|
| 1. | Upto S.S.L.C. | 8 (7.84) | 90 (45.46) |
| 2. | Graduates | 61 (59.80) | 74 (37.37) |
| 3. | Post Graduates | 23 (22.55) | 22 (11.11) |
| 4. | Technical | 10 (9.81) | 12 (6.06) |
| | **Total** | **102 (100)** | **198 (100)** |

*Source:* Primary data (Figures in parentheses indicate the percentage)

It is apparent from Table 6.3, that out of 102 sample respondents in non-agricultural sector, about 10 (9.81%) have technical qualifications like, bachelor's degree or diploma in engineering, 23 (22.55%) are post graduates, 61 (59.80%) are graduates and 8 (7.84%) have SSLC qualification.

Further, it is also inferred from Table 6.3 that out of 198 sample respondents, who are the beneficiaries of the programme, about 12 (6.06%) have technical qualification, 22 (11.11%) are post-graduates, 74 (37.37%) are graduates and about 90 respondents (45.46%) have passed SSLC.

Thus it is concluded form the analysis that all the sample respondents are well educated and more than 90 per cent of them are graduates, post-graduates and possess technical qualifications in non-agricultural and agricultural sector respectively.

The respondents are classified on the basis of their marital status in Table 6.4.

**Table 6.4: Classification of the Respondents on the Basis of Their Marital Status**

| Sl. No. | Marital Status | Non-Agricultural Activities | Agriculture and Allied Activities |
|---|---|---|---|
| 1. | Married | 93 (91.18) | 182 (91.92) |
| 2. | Unmarried | 6 (5.88) | 10 (5.05) |
| 3. | Widow/Divorcee | 3 (2.94) | 6 (3.03) |
| | **Total** | **102 (100)** | **198 (100)** |

*Source:* Primary data (Figures in parentheses indicate the percentage)

Table 6.4 reveals that out of 102 sample respondents, 93 (91.18%) are married, 6 (5.88%) are unmarried, and 3 (2.94%) are widows/divorcees. It is also concluded from the Table 6.4 that out of 198 sample beneficiaries engaged in agricultural and allied activities, 182 (91.92%) are married, 10 (5.05%) are unmarried and about 6 (3.03%) of them are widows/divorcees in the study area.

Thus, it could be concluded that more than 90 per cent of the sample beneficiaries in both agricultural and non-agricultural sector in the study area are married.

Caste wise classification of the sample respondents is given in Table 6.5.

**Table 6.5: Caste-wise Classification of the Respondents**

| Sl. No. | Caste | Non-Agricultural Activities | Agriculture and Allied Activities |
|---|---|---|---|
| 1. | OC | 19 (18.63) | 33 (16.67) |
| 2. | BC/MBC | 54 (52.94) | 142 (71.72) |
| 3. | SC/ST | 29 (28.43) | 23 (11.61) |
| | **Total** | **102 (100)** | **198 (100)** |

*Source:* Primary data (Figures in parentheses indicate the percentage)

Table 6.5, clearly shows the caste-wise classification of the sample respondents in the study area. Out of 102 sample respondents in non-agricultural sector, 19 (18.63%) belong to other castes (OC), 54 (52.94%) to backward and most backward classes (BC/MBC) and 29 (28.43%) belong to scheduled caste and scheduled tribes (SC/ST). Further, it is also observed that among the 198 respondents in agricultural and allied sector, 142 (71.72%) belong to BC/MBC, 33 (16.67%) of them belong to other classes and 23 (11.61%) of them are SC/ST in the study area.

The distribution of sample respondents based on religion is given in Table 6.6.

Table 6.6 clearly exhibits that out of 102 respondents, 44 (43.14%) are Hindus, 43 (42.71%) are Christians and 15 (14.70%) are Muslims.

It is further understood that out of 198 respondents, 120 (60.61%) are Christians, 68 (34.34%) are Hindus and 10 (5.05%) are Muslims.

**Table 6.6: Religion-wise Classification of the Sample Beneficiaries**

| Sl. No. | Religion | Non-Agricultural Activities | Agriculture and Allied Activities |
|---|---|---|---|
| 1. | Hindu | 44 (43.14) | 68 (34.34) |
| 2. | Muslim | 15 (14.70) | 10 (5.05) |
| 3. | Christian | 43 (42.16) | 120 (60.61) |
| | **Total** | **102 (100)** | **198 (100)** |

*Source:* Primary data (Figures in parentheses indicate the percentage)

Thus it could be concluded that majority of the respondents are Christians in the study area.

The distribution of respondents according to their family size is given in Table 6.7.

**Table 6.7: Family Size of the Sample Beneficiaries**

| Sl. No. | Family Size | Non-Agricultural Activities | Agriculture and Allied Activities |
|---|---|---|---|
| 1. | Below 3 members | 32 (31.37) | 72 (36.36) |
| 2. | 3-5 members | 64 (62.75) | 97 (48.99) |
| 3. | 5 members and above | 6 (5.88) | 29 (14.65) |
| | **Total** | **102 (100)** | **198 (100)** |

*Source:* Primary data (Figures in parentheses indicate the percentage)

Table 6.7 clearly exhibits that out of 102 respondents in non-agricultural sector, 32 (31.37%) have below 3 members in the family, 64 (62.75%) have 3-5 members and 6 (5.88%) have 5 members and above in their family.

Further, it is explained that, out of 198 respondents in agricultural and allied sectors, 72 (36.36%) have below 3 members in the family, 97 (48.99%) and 29 (14.65%) have 3 to 5 members and 5 and above in their family.

Classification of the respondents according to the Type of family is presented in Table 6.8.

**Table 6.8: Classification of the Respondents According to the Type of Family**

| Sl. No. | Type of Family | Non-Agricultural Activities | Agriculture and Allied Activities |
|---|---|---|---|
| 1. | Joint Family | 78 (76.47) | 162 (81.82) |
| 2. | Nuclear Family | 24 (23.53) | 36 (18.18) |
| | **Total** | **102 (100)** | **198 (100)** |

*Source:* Primary data (Figures in parentheses indicate the percentage)

It is inferred from Table 6.8 that out of 102 respondents in non-agricultural sector, 78 (76.47%) belong to joint family and 24 (23.53%) have nuclear family. Out of 198 respondents from agricultural and allied sector concerned 162 (81.82%) have joint family and about 36 (18.18%) have nuclear family respectively.

The respondents have been classified into three groups based on their monthly income and shown in Table 6.9.

**Table 6.9: Classification of Monthly Income of the Beneficiaries**

| Sl. No. | Monthly Income (in Rs.) | Non-Agricultural Activities | Agriculture and Allied Activities |
|---|---|---|---|
| 1. | Below 5000 | 8 (7.84) | 22 (11.11) |
| 2. | 5000-10000 | 78 (76.47) | 153 (77.27) |
| 3. | 10000 and above | 16 (15.69) | 23 (11.62) |
| | **Total** | **102 (100)** | **198 (100)** |

*Source:* Primary data (Figures in parentheses indicate the percentage)

It is observed from Table 6.9 that out of 102 respondents in non-agricultural sector, 78 (76.47%) come under the category of Rs. 5,000 - Rs. 10,000. 16 (15.69%) have monthly income of Rs. 10,000 and above and 8 (7.84%) have income below Rs. 5,000.

On the other hand it is observed that among 198 respondents, 153 (77.27%) come under the monthly income category of Rs. 5,000 - Rs. 10,000. 23 (11.62%) and 22 (11.11%) come under the monthly income category of Rs. 10000 and above and below Rs. 5,000 respectively.

Distribution of the sample respondents, based on the reason for getting loan are presented in Table 6.10.

**Table: 6.10: Reasons for Getting Loan**

| Sl. No. | Reasons | Non-Agricultural Activities | Agriculture and Allied Activities |
|---|---|---|---|
| 1. | Lack of employment opportunities | 62 (60.78) | 126 (63.64) |
| 2. | Previous employment was not profitable | 10 (9.81) | 18 (9.09) |
| 3. | Opportunity to use own skills | 9 (8.82) | 8 (4.04) |
| 4. | Encouragement given by others | 7 (6.86) | 12 (6.06) |
| 5. | Alternatives of Government subsidy | 13 (12.75) | 32 (16.16) |
| 6. | Any other reason | 1 (0.98) | 2 (1.01) |
| | **Total** | **102 (100)** | **198 (100)** |

*Source:* Primary data (Figures in parentheses indicate the percentage)

From Table 6.10 it is inferred that in the case of non-agricultural activities, out of 102 respondents, for the majority of 62 (60.78%) the reason for getting loan is lack of employment opportunity followed by 13 (12.75%) with reason that loan is an alternative to Government subsidy, for 10 (9.81%) it was previous employment was not profitable, for 9

(8.82%) to take the opportunity to use own skills, for 7 (6.86%) encouragement given by others and only 1 (0.98%) of them had other reasons for getting loan.

Out of 198 respondents from the sector of agriculture and allied activities, for 126 respondents (63.64%) the reason for getting loan is lack of employment opportunities, followed by 32 (16.16%) with the reason alternative of government subsidy, for 18 (9.09%) it is previous employment was not profitable, for 12 (6.06%) it is encouragement given by others, for 8 respondents (4.04%) the reason is to make opportunity to use own skills and only 2 respondents (1.01%) have other reasons for getting loan.

From Table 6.11, it is revealed that, out of the 102 respondents engaged in non-agricultural activities, majority of 37 (36.27%) have their source of information about the scheme from voluntary organisation, 24(23.53%) through friends/relatives, 23 (22.55%) through radio/TV and 18 (17.65%) had their information from newspapers.

Table 6.11 presents the sources of information about the schemes.

**Table 6.11: Sources of Information About the Schemes Under Lead Bank**

| Sl. No. | Sources | Non-Agricultural Activities | Agriculture and Allied Activities |
|---|---|---|---|
| 1. | Newspapers | 18 (17.65) | 8 (4.04) |
| 2. | Radio/TV | 23 (22.55) | 12 (6.06) |
| 3. | Friends/Relatives | 24 (23.53) | 93 (46.97) |
| 4. | Voluntary Organisations | 37 (36.27) | 85 (42.93) |
| | **Total** | **102 (100)** | **198 (100)** |

*Source:* Primary data (Figures in parentheses indicate the percentage)

In the case of agricultural and allied activities, out of 198 sample respondents, majority of 93 (46.97%) had their information about the scheme was through friends/relatives, 85 (42.93%) through voluntary organisation, 12 (6.06%) through radio/TV and only 8 (4.04%) had their information from newspaper.

Table 6.12 shows the reason for selecting the present venture.

**Table 6.12: Reasons for Selecting the Present Venture**

| Sl. No. | Reasons | Non-Agricultural Activities | Agriculture and Allied Activities |
|---|---|---|---|
| 1. | Previous experience | 12 (11.77) | 8 (4.04) |
| 2. | Demand for the product | 14 (13.73) | 6 (3.03) |
| 3. | Influence of location | 13 (12.74) | 53 (26.77) |
| 4. | Influence of the training | 26 (25.49) | 79 (39.90) |
| 5. | Desire to avail of the maximum loan amount | 14 (13.73) | 32 (16.16) |
| 6. | Family business extension | 13 (12.74) | 12 (6.06) |
| 7. | Any other | 10 (9.80) | 8 (4.04) |
| | **Total** | **102 (100)** | **198 (100)** |

*Source:* Primary data (Figures in parentheses indicate the percentage.

From Table 6.12, it is seen that in the case of non-agricultural activities, out of 102 respondents, for 26 respondents (25.49%) the reason for selecting their present venture was influence of training, for 14 (13.73%) it was demand for product and desire to avail the maximum loan amount, for 13 (12.74%) the reason was family business extension and influence of location.

In the case of agricultural and allied activities, out of 198 sample respondents, for 79 respondents (39.90%) the reason for selecting their present venture was influence of training, for 53 (26.77%) it was influence of location, for 32 (16.16%) the reason was desire to avail the maximum loan amount and for 12 (6.06%) the reason was family business extension.

Table 6.13 shows the project report prepared for applying for loan.

**Table 6.13: Project Report Preparation**

| Sl. No. | Method of Preparation | Non-Agricultural Activities | Agriculture and Allied Activities |
|---|---|---|---|
| 1. | By beneficiary himself | 2<br>(1.96) | 1<br>(0.51) |
| 2. | Copying the existing reports | 4<br>(3.92) | 3<br>(1.51) |
| 3. | By others on the basis of suggestions given by the beneficiary | 96<br>(94.12) | 194<br>(97.98) |
| | **Total** | **102**<br>**(100)** | **198**<br>**(100)** |

*Source:* Primary data (Figures in parentheses indicate the percentage).

Table 6.13 depicts that in the case of non-agricultural activities, out of 102 sample respondents, 96 (94.12%) get their project report prepared by others on the basis of suggestions given by the beneficiary, 4 (3.92%) get project report prepared by copying the existing reports and 2 respondents (1.96%) prepared their report themselves.

In the case of agricultural and allied activities, out of 198 respondents, 194 (97.98%) got their project report prepared by others, on the basis of suggestions given by the beneficiary, 3 (1.51%) prepared their report by copying the existing reports and only 1 (0.57%) prepared the report themselves.

Table 6.14 shows the details of whether entire the loan amount applied for was received or not.

**Table 6.14: Whether Entire Amount Applied for Loan was Received**

| Sl. No. | Whether Entire Loan was received | Non-Agricultural Activities | Agriculture and Allied Activities |
|---|---|---|---|
| 1. | Yes | 6 (5.88) | 22 (11.11) |
| 2. | No | 96 (94.12) | 176 (88.89) |
| | **Total** | **102 (100)** | **198 (100)** |

*Source:* Primary data (Figures in parentheses indicate the percentage)

It is clearly evident from Table 6.14 that in the case of non-agricultural activities, out of 102 respondents, 96 (94.12%) did not receive the entire amount applied as loan whereas only 6 (5.88%) received the entire amount of loan. In the case of agricultural and allied activities, out of 198 respondents, 176 (88.89%) did not receive the entire amount of loan while only 22 (11.11%) received the entire amount of loan applied by the respondents.

## INCOME ASSET AND EMPLOYMENT GENERATION

### Income Generation

The assets, financed under the Lead Bank Scheme, can be expected to produce returns within a period of one year from the commencement of the project and commercialization of the produce or services. The success of the scheme lies in its ability to generate additional income to the beneficiaries, resulting in a chain of reinvestment returns, from the additional assets created. In this section, the impact of government sponsored programmes under the Lead Bank Scheme, on the beneficiaries is identified, in terms of the additional income-generating capacity of the families of the borrowers.

**Family Asset Positions Before and After Joining the Government Sponsored Programme Under the Lead Bank Scheme**

Table 6.15 gives the distribution of assets among the four different asset groups and shows the average family assets of the respondents before and after getting financial assistance under Government sponsored programmes under the Lead Bank Scheme.

**Table 6.15: Classification of Family Assets Before and After Joining the Government Sponsored Programme Under Lead Bank Scheme**

| Sl. No. | Asset Groups (Rs.) | No. of Beneficiaries | Pre-loan Period | Post-loan Period | Percentage of Increase | t-value |
|---|---|---|---|---|---|---|
| | | | Average Per Capita Income (Rs.) | Average Per Capita Income (Rs.) | | |
| 1. | Below 20,000 | 94 | 17,289.99 | 27,199.22 | 58.15 | 5.42* |
| 2. | 20000-30000 | 124 | 22,453.65 | 37,214.15 | 66.21 | 5.21* |
| 3. | 30000-40000 | 51 | 39,863.14 | 59,563.43 | 50.14 | 4.21* |
| 4. | 40000 and above | 31 | 45,624.16 | 67,893.15 | 49.82 | 5.22* |
| | Overall | 300 | 28,933.42 | 41,218.24 | 48.54 | 5.72* |

*Source:* Computed data
*Note:* *Significant at 5 per cent level.

It could be seen from Table 6.15 that there has been an increase in the asset position of the beneficiaries after getting financial assistance through Government sponsored programmes under Lead Bank Scheme, The percentage of increase in assets, is found to be the highest i.e, 66.21 per cent, for those in the asset group of Rs. 20,000 to Rs. 30,000. It is followed by 58.15 per cent for the asset group below Rs. 20,000. An increase of 50.14 per cent and 49.82 per cent in asset position is found in the asset groups of Rs. 30,000 Rs. 40,000 and above Rs. 40,000 respectively. It reveals that the government- sponsored programme under the Lead Bank Scheme is successful in promoting the standard of living of the borrowers' families through improvement in their asset position.

Table 6.16 gives the changes in family assets during pre-loan and post-loan periods for different types of activities.

**Table 6.16: Activity-wise Changes in Family Assets during Pre-loan and Post-loan Periods**

| Sl. No. | Activity | No. of Benefi-ciaries | Pre-loan Period | Post-loan Period | Percentage of Increase | t-value |
|---|---|---|---|---|---|---|
| | | | Average Per Capita Income (Rs.) | Average Per Capita Income (Rs.) | | |
| 1. | Non-agricultural activities | 102 | 32,164.21 | 49,218.15 | 54.21 | 3.21* |
| 2. | Agriculture and allied activities | 198 | 22,938.15 | 36,483.61 | 50.09 | 4.24* |
| | Overall | 300 | 25,319.21 | 37,214.41 | 53.21 | 4.26* |

*Source:* Computed data

*Note:* *Significant at 5 per cent level

The addition to assets is found to vary for those engaged in different types of activities. In absolute terms, the increase in the assets is found to be higher in non-agricultural activities and lower in agricultural and allied activities. Percentage-wise, there is 54.21 per cent increase in the asset position for those engaged in non-agricultural activities followed by 50.09 per cent increase in agricultural and allied activities of the families of the beneficiaries.

### *Generation of Additional Mandays of Employment*

The size of employment generated is measured in terms of average mandays within the family of the four income groups, in order to identify the principal beneficiaries of the government sponsored programme under the Lead Bank Scheme.

Table 6.17 shows the number of additional mandays of employment generated by government-sponsored programmes under the Lead Bank Scheme among different income groups.

**Table 6.17: Additional Mandays of Employment Generated by Government Sponsored Programmes in Different Income Groups**

| Sl. No. | Per capita Income-wise Classification (Rs.) | Number of Beneficiaries | Average Mandays Generated within the Family | Average Mandays Generated with Regard to Hired Hands |
|---|---|---|---|---|
| 1. | Below 2000 | 81 | 313 | 229 |
| 2. | 2000 - 4000 | 185 | 321 | 319 |
| 3. | 4000 - 6000 | 28 | 269 | 256 |
| 4. | 6000 and above | 6 | 316 | 246 |
| | **Overall** | **300** | **294** | **264** |

*Source:* Computed data

Regarding average mandays of employment created within the family, it was found to vary from 269 to 321. The highest average mandays of employment was found among the income group Rs. 2,000 to Rs. 4,000 followed by the income group of Rs. 6,000 and above.

Employment generated among the people, other than family members on hired basis, was found to vary between 229 mandays and 319 mandays. The average number of mandays generated was found to be the highest among the income group of Rs. 2,000 - Rs. 4,000 followed by the income group Rs. 4,000 - Rs. 6,000.

Table 6.18 gives the activity-wise employment pattern and labour generated under various government-sponsored programmes under Lead Bank Scheme.

The Table 6.18 shows that among the different activities undertaken by the Government-sponsored programmes, under the Lead Bank Scheme, beneficiaries of non-agricultural activities have generated more number of mandays both within the family and with hired labourers. In the case of other activities, the average days of employment is less and range between 250 and 298 days only.

**Table 6.18: Activity-wise Employment Generated Under Various Government Sponsored Programmes**

| Sl. No. | Activities | Number of Beneficiaries | Average Mandays Among Family Members | Average Mandays Generated with Regard to Hired Hands |
|---|---|---|---|---|
| 1. | Non-agricultural activities | 102 | 301 | 294 |
| 2. | Agriculture and allied activities | 198 | 298 | 250 |
| | **Overall** | **300** | **287** | **264** |

*Source:* Computed data

## FACTORS INFLUENCING THE REPAYMENT OF LOAN

In this section, an attempt has been made to analyse the repayment performance of loan by the beneficiaries of the government sponsored programmes under the Lead Bank Scheme. The repayment schedule is determined in respect of term loan component. The government sponsored programmes under the Lead Bank Scheme stipulate that the period of repayment of term loan component shall be three to seven years with a moratorium period of 6 to 18 months. In order to identify the factors which influence the repayment of loan in the study area, data has been collected regarding the loan amount received, the net income received from the venture (trade), number of instalments and annual family income including other sources of each activity namely, non-agricultural activities and agricultural and allied activities.

### Analytical Framework

In order to identify the factors, which influence the amount of loan repayment with respect to non-agricultural activities, agricultural and allied activities and overall, the log linear regression model is used. In this regression model, annual repaid amount in rupees (*Y*) is treated as a dependent variable and the following influencing factors are treated as independent variables.

1. Loan amount received, (in rupees) ($x_1$)
2. Annual net income received from the venture ($x_2$)
3. Annual family income including other sources ($x_3$)
4. Number of instalments ($x_4$)

In the linear regression model, one dependent variable and four independent variables are included in the form given below:

$$\text{Log } Y\ \beta_0 + \beta_1 \log x_1 + \beta_2 \log x_2 + \log x_3 + \log x_4 + U \quad ...6.1$$

where,

$Y$ is annual repaid amount in rupees

$x_1$ is loan amount received in rupees

$x_2$ is annual net income received from the venture (in rupees)

$x_3$ is annual family income including other sources (in rupees)

$x_4$ is number of installments

U refers to disturbance term, and

$\beta_0, \beta_1, \ldots \beta_4$ are the parameters to be estimated.

The above model (6.1) was estimated by the method of least squares, for each activity separately. The computed results are presented in Table 6.19.

In the case of non-agricultural activities, all the four variables are jointly responsible for 99 per cent variations in the repayment of loan. The co-efficients of the amount of loan received and the number of instalments are statistically significant at 5 per cent level. The variable amount of loan received is positively related to the repayment whereas the variable 'the number of instalments' is negatively related to it. It indicates that an additional percentage of the amount of loan received could increase the repayment amount by 0.98 per cent. In the case of the number of instalments an addition made to this variable is capable of decreasing the repayment amount by 0.99 per cent.

**Table 6.19: Estimated values of the regression co-efficient**

| Variables | Parameter Estimates | | Overall |
|---|---|---|---|
| | Non-agricultural Activities | Agricultural and Allied Activities | |
| Intercept | 2.92 | 4.16 | 4.84 |
| log $X_1$ | 0.98*<br>(38.19) | 0.88*<br>(7.71) | 0.68*<br>(4.22) |
| log $X_2$ | -0.98<br>(-0.842) | 0.009<br>(0.022) | 0.0009<br>(0.018) |
| log $X_3$ | -0.008<br>(-0.27) | -0.08<br>(-0.097) | 0.08*<br>(2.79) |
| log $X_4$ | -0.99*<br>(-17.24) | -0.98*<br>(-5.22) | 0.98*<br>(5.37) |
| $R^2$<br>*t*-value | 0.98<br>397.12 | 0.76<br>22.16 | 0.66<br>8.99 |
| Sample Size | 102 | 198 | 300 |

*Source:* Computed Data. (Figures in parentheses are the *t* values)

*Note:* *Indicates that the co-efficients are statistically significant at 5 per cent level.

In the case of agricultural and allied activities, the same two co-efficients are statistically significant at 5 per cent level. In this category, the variable 'amount of loan received by the beneficiaries' shows a positive relation to the repayment of loan. The co-efficient of variable, 'the number of instalments' shows negative relation to it. The $R^2$ value indicates that all the explanatory variables, jointly account for about 76 per cent responsibility in the repayment.

In the case of overall activities, three out of four variables are statistically significant at 5 per cent level. The explanatory variables, together account for 66 per cent variations in the repayment amount. The amount of loan received and annual family income have a positive effect on the repayment amount of loan. It means that one percent increase in these variables is capable of increasing repayment by 0.68 per cent showing a negative effect on 'the repayment of loan'. As per the '*t*'-value given in Table 6.7 in all the three categories, the regression model is found to be significant at one per cent level.

Thus, it may be concluded from the above results, that in all the three categories, namely, non-agricultural activities, agricultural and allied activities and overall activities, the two variables namely 'the amount of loan received' and 'the number of installments', have the same influence on the repayment of loan under government-sponsored programme under the Lead Bank Scheme. In the case of overall activities, in addition to those two variables, the variable, 'annual family income' is also a significant one, influencing the repayment of loan under government-sponsored programmes under the Lead Bank Scheme.

## RECOVERY PERFORMANCE

Recovery performance assumes greater significance as it involves utilization of public money for sanctioning of loans. Recovery performance is an indicator of the successful functioning of the scheme and it enables the financial institutions to recycle the money, to cover more number of eligible beneficiaries. The government-sponsored programmes under the Lead Bank Scheme, come under the poverty alleviation schemes and the performance of the scheme in terms of coverage and recovery, helps in improving and comparing its performance with schemes that are in vogue. Moreover, recovery performance needs to be analysed since the loan sanctioning authority is given to banks whereas identification of beneficiaries for the government-sponsored programmes under the Lead Bank Scheme is done by the government.

The growing incidence of defaults in repayment of loans under government-sponsored programmes under the Lead Bank Scheme, has attracted the attention of bankers and authorities concerned, prompting them to analyse the causes for such poor performance and to find out ways for improving recovery performance.

To study the recovery performance, information was collected regarding the amount of loan sanctioned, date of sanctioning, moratorium period given and number of instalments paid, from the records of the banks. For the purpose of analysing recovery performance, 6 banks were selected and information regarding demand and collection was collected for a period of ten years from 1999-2000 to 2008-09. Data on recovery has been calculated by demand collection balance method.

Demand (D) as on 31.03.2009

Collection (C) as on 31.03.2009

Overdue (O) as on 31.03.2009

The interest due upto 31.03.2009 is also added to arrive at demand (D).

The amount paid upto 31.03.2009 by the borrowers is added to the subsidy interest accrued is taken as 'amount collected'. Overdue is calculated by deducting the amount collected(C) from demand (D).

**Framework of Analysis**

The percentage of recovery in calculated by using the formula:

$$R = \frac{C}{D} \times 100 \qquad \ldots (6.2)$$

where,

$R$ = Recovery percentage

$C$ = Collected amount and

$D$ = Demand

**Trend and Growth of Recovery Performance**

In order to examine the growth of demand, collection and overdue and its stability over the period of ten years from 1999-2000 to 2008-2009, the arithmetic mean ($\bar{X}$) and co-efficient of variation (C.V) of the following formula was used.

$$\text{Co-efficient of Variation (\%)} = \frac{S.D}{X} \times 100 \qquad \ldots (6.3)$$

where

$S.D$ = Standard deviation

$\bar{X}$ = Mean

The trend and compound growth rates are computed for demand, collection and overdue, by adopting the semi-log trend model as given below:

$$\text{Log } Y = a + bt \qquad \ldots (6.4)$$

where

$Y$ = variable

$t$ = Time variable

and '$a$' and '$b$' are the parameters to be estimated.

The above model (6.4) was estimated by the method of least squares. The compound growth rate was calculated by using the following formula:

$$\text{Compound Growth Rate (\%)} = [\text{Anti log } b - 1] \times 100 \qquad \ldots (6.5)$$

The data pertaining to government-sponsored programmes regarding demand, collection, recovery percentage, overdue and overdue percentage of the State Bank of India in Kanyakumari district is presented in Table 6.20.

It is inferred from Table 6.20 that the demand in State Bank of India ranged between Rs. 20.18 lakhs and Rs. 114.18 lakhs during the study period. The data shows an increase in demand position each year and the overall demand during the study period was Rs. 444.00 lakhs. The collection from the beneficiaries was encouraging and the overall recovery rate was 77.17 per cent. The highest recovery rate of 98.31 per cent was achieved in the year 2006-2007. The lowest recovery rate of 48.72 per cent was found during the year 2004-2005.

**Table 6.20: Recovery Performance of State Bank of India (SBI) During the Period from 1999-2000 to 2008-09**

*(Rs. in Lakhs)*

| Sl. No. | Year | Demand | Collection | Recovery Percentage | Overdue | Overdue Percentage |
|---|---|---|---|---|---|---|
| 1. | 1999-2000 | 20.18 | 19.05 | 94.40 | 1.13 | 5.60 |
| 2. | 2000-2001 | 21.90 | 19.10 | 87.21 | 2.80 | 12.79 |
| 3. | 2001-2002 | 24.62 | 23.67 | 96.14 | 0.95 | 3.86 |
| 4. | 2002-2003 | 24.74 | 21.32 | 86.18 | 3.42 | 13.82 |
| 5. | 2003-2004 | 30.76 | 23.79 | 77.34 | 6.97 | 22.67 |
| 6. | 2004-2005 | 37.13 | 18.09 | 48.72 | 19.04 | 51.28 |
| 7. | 2005-2006 | 41.87 | 31.44 | 75.09 | 10.43 | 24.91 |
| 8. | 2006-2007 | 58.68 | 57.69 | 98.31 | 0.99 | 1.69 |
| 9. | 2007-2008 | 69.94 | 68.51 | 97.95 | 1.43 | 2.05 |
| 10. | 2008-2009 | 114.18 | 59.95 | 52.50 | 54.23 | 47.46 |
| | **Overall** | **444.00** | **342.61** | **77.17** | **101.39** | **22.83** |

*Source:* Compiled from the Annual Credit plan of IOB, Kanyakumari District, (Lead Bank) from 1999-2000 to 2008-2009.

The overdue of Rs. 54.23 lakhs during 2008-09, followed by Rs. 19.04 lakhs during 2004-05, were the highest during the study period. During the rest of the study period, it ranged between Rs. 0.95 lakhs and Rs. 54.23 lakhs. The overdue percentage of 51.28 per cent during 2004-05 was the highest during the study period. During the rest of the study period, the overdue percentage ranged between 1.69 per cent and 47.46 per cent.

The following Table 6.21 presents the average and stability of demand, collection and overdue of government-sponsored schemes in State Bank of India in Kanyakumari district.

Table 6.21 indicates that the average amount of demand, collection and overdue was Rs. 44.40 lakhs, Rs. 34.26 lakhs and Rs. 10.14 lakhs respectively. A fluctuation of 62.91 per cent was found in overdue whereas it was 66.49 per cent and 59.59 per cent in demand and collection respectively.

**Table 6.21: Average and Stability of Demand, Collection and Overdue of State Bank of India in Kanyakumari District During the Period from 1999-2000 to 2008-09**

(*Rs. in Lakhs*)

| Sl. No. | Particulars | Demand | Collection | Overdue |
|---|---|---|---|---|
| 1. | Mean | 44.40 | 34.26 | 10.14 |
| 2. | S.D | 29.52 | 19.73 | 16.52 |
| 3. | C.V (%) | 66.49 | 59.59 | 62.91 |

*Source:* Computed data.

The computed results of trend and growth rates in demand, collection and overdue of State Bank of India in Kanyakumari district are given in Table 6.22.

**Table 6.22: Trend and Growth of Demand, Collection and Overdue of State Bank of India in Kanyakumari District**

| Sl. No. | Particulars | Trend co-efficient | | | CGR (%) |
|---|---|---|---|---|---|
| | | a | b | $\bar{R}^2$ | |
| 1. | Demand | 2.69 | 0.16* (36.28) | 0.98 | 16.97 |
| 2. | Collection | 2.51 | 0.16* (36.42) | 0.98 | 16.97 |
| 3. | Overdue | 0.61 | 0.18* (8.49) | 0.88 | 21.43 |

*Source:* Computed data. (Figures in the parentheses are *t* - value)

*Note:* *Indicates that the trend co-efficient are statistically significant at 5 per cent level.

It is inferred from the above table, that the trend coefficient of demand, collection and overdue are statistically significant at 5 per cent level. The demand, collection and overdue show an increase, at the rate of 0.16 per cent, 0.16 per cent and 0.18 per cent respectively. The growth was found to be high in overdue with 21.43 per cent, followed by demand and collection with 16.97 per cent and 16.97 per cent respectively.

The recovery performance of Canara Bank in respect of government-sponsored programmes is presented in the following Table 6.23.

**Table 6.23: Recovery Performance of Canara Bank (CB) During the Period from 1999-2000 to 2008-09**

*(Rs. in Lakhs)*

| Sl. No. | Year | Demand | Collection | Recovery Percentage | Overdue | Overdue Percentage |
|---|---|---|---|---|---|---|
| 1. | 1999-2000 | 32.80 | 18.70 | 57.01 | 14.10 | 42.99 |
| 2. | 2000-2001 | 26.44 | 23.48 | 88.80 | 2.96 | 11.20 |
| 3. | 2001-2002 | 27.17 | 26.19 | 96.39 | 0.98 | 3.61 |
| 4. | 2002-2003 | 28.17 | 27.42 | 97.34 | 0.75 | 2.66 |
| 5. | 2003-2004 | 33.60 | 32.69 | 97.29 | 0.91 | 2.71 |
| 6. | 2004-2005 | 41.23 | 40.95 | 99.32 | 0.28 | 0.68 |
| 7. | 2005-2006 | 70.99 | 70.45 | 99.24 | 0.54 | 0.76 |
| 8. | 2006-2007 | 99.16 | 92.43 | 93.21 | 6.73 | 6.79 |
| 9. | 2007-2008 | 116.37 | 58.25 | 50.08 | 58.12 | 49.94 |
| 10. | 2008-2009 | 116.49 | 110.50 | 94.86 | 5.99 | 5.14 |
| | **Overall** | **592.42** | **501.06** | **84.58** | **91.36** | **15.42** |

*Source:* Compiled from the Annual Credit plan of IOB, Kanyakumari District, (Lead Bank) from 1999-2000 to 2008-2009.

It is inferred from Table 6.23 that the Canara Bank's demand shows an upward trend in disbursing loans to government-sponsored programmes under the Lead Bank Scheme. The overall demand was Rs. 592.42 lakhs while the overall collection stood at Rs. 501.06 lakhs during the period of study. The study period shows that the lowest recovery was 50.08 per cent during 2007-08. The highest recovery performance was 99.32 per cent during 2004-05. Thus it is seen that during the period of study the recovery percentage ranged between 50.08 to 99.32.

The overdue percentage was 0.68 per cent during 2004-05, which is the lowest and 49.94 per cent during 2007-08 which is the highest in the study period. The overall overdue position stood at 15.42 per cent.

The following Table 6.24 presents the average and stability of demand, collection and overdue of government-sponsored schemes of Canara Bank in Kanyakumari district.

**Table 6.24: Average and Stability of Demand, Collection and Overdue of Canara Bank in Kanyakumari District during the Period from 1999-2000 to 2008-09**

(*Rs. in Lakhs*)

| Sl. No. | Particulars | Demand | Collection | Overdue |
|---|---|---|---|---|
| 1. | Mean | 59.24 | 50.11 | 9.14 |
| 2. | S.D | 38.04 | 31.78 | 17.47 |
| 3. | C.V (%) | 64.21 | 63.42 | 91.13 |

*Source:* Computed data.

The above table shows that, the average amount of demand, collection and overdue during the study period was Rs. 59.24 lakhs, Rs. 50.11 lakhs and Rs. 9.14 lakhs respectively. It is inferred from the analysis that the variation was found to be high in overdue (91.13%) followed by collection and demand.

Table 6.25 shows, the computed results of trend and growth rates in demand, collection and overdue of Canara Bank in Kanyakumari district.

**Table 6.25: Trend and Growth of Demand, Collection and Overdue of Canara Bank in Kanyakumari District**

| Sl. No. | Particulars | Trend Co-efficient | | | CGR (%) |
|---|---|---|---|---|---|
| | | a | b | $\overline{R}^2$ | |
| 1. | Demand | 2.61 | 0.12* (9.56) | 0.92 | 10.74 |
| 2. | Collection | 2.41 | 0.14* (7.49) | 0.88 | 12.35 |
| 3. | Overdue | 0.39 | 0.18 (0.379) | 0.14 | 1.94 |

*Source:* Computed data. (Figures in the parentheses are t-value)

*Note:* *Indicates that the trend co-efficient are statistically significant at 5 per cent level.

It is inferred from the analysis that the demand and collection are statistically significant at 5 per cent level. The trend coefficient shows an increase of 0.12 per cent in demand, 0.14 per cent in collection and 0.18 per cent in overdue. The compound growth rate was found to be high in 'collection' with 12.35 per cent and it was 10.74 per cent in demand. The overdue growth rate was 1.94 per cent.

The recovery performance of Indian Overseas Bank in respect of government-sponsored programmes is shown in the following Table 6.26.

**Table 6.26: Recovery Performance of Indian Overseas Bank (IOB) During the Period from 1999-2000 to 2008-09**

*(Rs. in Lakhs)*

| Sl. No. | Year | Demand | Collection | Recovery Percentage | Overdue | Overdue Percentage |
|---|---|---|---|---|---|---|
| 1. | 1999-2000 | 31.85 | 29.12 | 91.43 | 2.73 | 8.57 |
| 2. | 2000-2001 | 34.87 | 34.50 | 98.94 | 0.37 | 1.06 |
| 3. | 2001-2002 | 38.03 | 36.56 | 96.13 | 1.47 | 3.87 |
| 4. | 2002-2003 | 40.47 | 35.99 | 88.93 | 4.48 | 11.06 |
| 5. | 2003-2004 | 41.06 | 40.10 | 97.66 | 0.96 | 2.44 |
| 6. | 2004-2005 | 51.84 | 50.66 | 97.72 | 1.18 | 2.28 |
| 7. | 2005-2006 | 104.09 | 101.92 | 97.92 | 2.17 | 2.08 |
| 8. | 2006-2007 | 134.66 | 131.17 | 97.41 | 3.49 | 2.59 |
| 9. | 2007-2008 | 162.42 | 156.87 | 96.58 | 5.55 | 3.42 |
| 10. | 2008-2009 | 206.09 | 158.31 | 76.82 | 47.78 | 23.18 |
| | **Overall** | **845.38** | **775.20** | **91.70** | **70.18** | **8.30** |

*Source:* Compiled from the Annual Credit plan of IOB, Kanyakumari District, (Lead Bank) from 1999-2000 to 2008-2009.

The recovery performance of IOB given in Table 6.26, shows that the overall demand during the study period from 1999-2000 to 2008-09 was Rs. 845.38 lakhs. The overall recovery percentage for the study period was 91.70. The recovery percentage varies 76.82 per cent to 98.94 per cent. The overdue percentage of 1.06 during 2000-01 was the lowest during the period of study. Among the ten years of the study period, overdue percentages of two years viz., 2002-03 and 2008-09 were higher than 10 per cent.

Table 6.27 presents the average and stability of demand, collection and overdue of government-sponsored schemes in Indian Overseas Bank in Kanyakumari district.

**Table 6.27: Average and Stability of Demand, Collection and Overdue of Indian Overseas Bank in Kanyakumari District During the Period from 1999-2000 to 2008-09**

**(*Rs. in Lakhs*)**

| Sl. No. | Particulars | Demand | Collection | Overdue |
|---|---|---|---|---|
| 1. | Mean | 84.54 | 77.52 | 7.02 |
| 2. | S.D | 63.28 | 53.76 | 12.42 |
| 3. | C.V (%) | 74.85 | 69.35 | 76.92 |

*Source:* Computed data.

It is inferred from Table 6.27 that the average amount of demand, collection and overdue were Rs. 84.54 lakhs, Rs. 77.52 lakhs and 7.02 lakhs respectively. It is observed that a high fluctuation was found in overdue, when compared to demand and collection.

The computed results of trend and growth rates in demand, collection and overdue of Indian Overseas Bank in Kanyakumari district are given in Table 6.28.

It is inferred from Table 6.28, that the trend coefficient of demand and collection are statistically significant at 5 per cent level. It is found that demand and collection are increasing at the rate of 0.13 per cent and 0.14 per cent. The compound growth rate percentage was high in collection than in demand. The overdue compound growth rate was 6.46 per cent.

**Table 6.28: Trend and Growth of Demand, Collection and Overdue of Indian Overseas Bank in Kanyakumari District**

| Sl. No. | Particulars | Trend co-efficient | | | CGR (%) |
|---|---|---|---|---|---|
| | | a | b | $\bar{R}^2$ | |
| 1. | Demand | 2.45 | 0.13* (4.59) | 0.72 | 11.82 |
| 2. | Collection | 2.28 | 0.14* (3.39) | 0.58 | 12.24 |
| 3. | Overdue | 0.49 | 0.08 (0.97) | 0.002 | 6.46 |

*Source:* Computed data. (Figures in the parentheses are t-value)

*Note:* *Indicates that the trend co-efficient are statistically significant at 5 percent level.

The recovery performance of Indian Bank in respect of government-sponsored programmes is shown in the following Table 6.29.

**Table 6.29: Recovery Performance of Indian Bank during the Period from 1999-2000 to 2008-09**

***(Rs. in Lakhs)***

| Sl. No. | Year | Demand | Collection | Recovery Percentage | Overdue | Overdue Percentage |
|---|---|---|---|---|---|---|
| 1. | 1999-2000 | 5.34 | 2.98 | 55.81 | 2.36 | 44.19 |
| 2. | 2000-2001 | 4.34 | 3.75 | 86.41 | 0.59 | 13.59 |
| 3. | 2001-2002 | 4.58 | 4.42 | 96.51 | 0.16 | 3.49 |
| 4. | 2002-2003 | 5.13 | 5.02 | 97.86 | 0.11 | 2.14 |
| 5. | 2003-2004 | 4.57 | 4.26 | 93.22 | 0.31 | 6.78 |
| 6. | 2004-2005 | 5.32 | 5.02 | 94.36 | 0.30 | 5.64 |
| 7. | 2005-2006 | 14.00 | 12.90 | 92.14 | 1.10 | 7.86 |
| 8. | 2006-2007 | 16.99 | 16.76 | 98.65 | 0.23 | 1.35 |
| 9. | 2007-2008 | 21.25 | 20.49 | 96.42 | 0.76 | 3.58 |
| 10. | 2008-2009 | 30.53 | 22.73 | 74.45 | 7.80 | 25.55 |
| | **Overall** | **112.05** | **98.33** | **87.75** | **13.72** | **12.24** |

*Source:* Compiled from the Annual Credit plan of IOB, Kanyakumari District, (Lead Bank) from 1999-2000 to 2008-2009.

It is understood from Table 6.29, that the overall demand position was Rs. 112.05 lakhs for the ten years of study from 1999-2000 to 2008-09. It shows an increasing trend in demand. The demand ranged between Rs. 4.34 lakhs and Rs. 30.53 lakhs during the period. The overall collection during the study period was Rs. 98.33 lakhs. The overall recovery rate stood at 87.75 per cent.

The overdue was the highest Rs. 7.80 lakhs during 2008-09. It ranged between Rs. 0.11 lakhs and Rs. 7.80 lakhs. The overall overdue was Rs. 13.72 lakhs. The overdue percentage was the highest during 1999-2000 (44.19%) and it was 1.35 per cent during 2006-07 which was the lowest. The overall overdue percentage stood at 12.24 per cent.

Table 6.30 shows the average and stability of demand, collection and overdue of government-sponsored scheme in Indian Bank in Kanyakumari district.

**Table 6.30: Average and Stability of Demand, Collection and Overdue of Indian Bank in Kanyakumari District During the Period from 1999-2000 to 2008-09**

***(Rs. in Lakhs)***

| Sl. No. | Particulars | Demand | Collection | Overdue |
|---|---|---|---|---|
| 1. | Mean | 11.20 | 9.83 | 1.37 |
| 2. | S.D | 9.17 | 7.69 | 2.36 |
| 3. | C.V (%) | 81.80 | 78.23 | 72.26 |

*Source:* Computed data.

From the above Table 6.30, it is calculated that the average amount of demand, collection and overdue were Rs. 11.20 lakhs, Rs. 9.83 lakhs and Rs. 1.37 lakhs respectively. As indicated by the coefficient of variation, less fluctuation was found in overdue and the percentage variation in 'demand' and 'collection' were 81.80 per cent and 78.23 per cent respectively during the period of study.

The following Table 6.31 shows the computed results of trend and growth rates in demand, collection and overdue of government-sponsored scheme in Indian Bank in Kanyakumari district.

**Table 6.31: Trend and Growth of Demand, Collection and Overdue of Indian Bank in Kanyakumari District**

| Sl. No. | Particulars | Trend Co-efficient | | | CGR (%) |
|---|---|---|---|---|---|
| | | a | b | $\bar{R}^2$ | |
| 1. | Demand | 2.92 | 0.08* (26.19) | 0.99 | 7.41 |
| 2. | Collection | 2.71 | 0.09* (24.15) | 0.99 | 8.58 |
| 3. | Overdue | 1.29 | 0.008 (0.61) | 0.09 | 0.79 |

*Source:* Computed data. (Figures in the parentheses are t-value)

*Note:* *Indicates that the trend co-efficient are statistically significant at 5 percent level.

The trend coefficients are increasing at the rate of 0.08 per cent, 0.09 per cent and 0.008 per cent respectively for demand, collection and overdue. The compound growth rate was found to be high in 'collection' with 8.58 per cent and with the highest of 7.41 per cent for demand. The overdue growth level was 0.79 per cent.

The recovery performance of Central Bank of India in respect of government-sponsored programmes is depicted in the following Table 6.32.

**Table 6.32: Recovery Performance of Central Bank of India During the Period from 1999-2000 to 2008-09**

**(*Rs. in Lakhs*)**

| Sl. No. | Year | Demand | Collection | Recovery Percentage | Overdue | Overdue Percentage |
|---|---|---|---|---|---|---|
| (1) | (2) | (3) | (4) | (5) | (6) | (7) |
| 1. | 1999-2000 | 2.69 | 1.10 | 40.89 | 1.59 | 59.11 |
| 2. | 2000-2001 | 3.01 | 2.41 | 80.07 | 0.60 | 19.93 |
| 3. | 2001-2002 | 3.51 | 3.47 | 98.86 | 0.04 | 1.14 |
| 4. | 2002-2003 | 4.07 | 2.68 | 65.85 | 1.39 | 34.15 |
| 5. | 2003-2004 | 3.97 | 2.51 | 63.22 | 1.46 | 36.78 |
| 6. | 2004-2005 | 4.53 | 2.05 | 45.25 | 2.48 | 54.75 |
| 7. | 2005-2006 | 9.12 | 8.10 | 88.82 | 1.02 | 11.18 |

*(Contd...)*

| (1) | (2) | (3) | (4) | (5) | (6) | (7) |
|---|---|---|---|---|---|---|
| 8. | 2006-2007 | 13.93 | 12.40 | 89.02 | 1.53 | 10.98 |
| 9. | 2007-2008 | 16.79 | 14.62 | 87.08 | 2.17 | 12.92 |
| 10. | 2008-2009 | 21.77 | 15.94 | 73.22 | 5.83 | 26.78 |
| | **Overall** | **83.39** | **65.28** | **78.28** | **18.11** | **21.72** |

*Source:* Compiled from the Annual Credit plan of IOB, Kanyakumari District, (Lead Bank) from 1999-2000 to 2008-2009.

Table 6.32 shows the recovery performance of the Central Bank of India. The demand shows an increasing trend each year and the collection too shows an upward trend during the period of study. The highest recovery performance registered during 2001-02 was 98.86 per cent. The overall recovery rate was 78.28 per cent. The overall overdue amount is Rs. 18.11 lakhs. The highest overdue percentage was 59.11 per cent during 1999-2000 and it was the lowest of 1.14 per cent during 2001-02. The overall overdue percentage stood at 21.72 per cent.

Table 6.33 presents the average and stability of demand, collection and overdue of government-sponsored schemes by the Union Bank of India in Kanyakumari district.

**Table 6.33: Average and Stability of Demand, Collection and Overdue of Union Bank of India in Kanyakumari District during the Period from 1999-2000 to 2008-09**

**(*Rs. in Lakhs*)**

| Sl. No. | Particulars | Demand | Collection | Overdue |
|---|---|---|---|---|
| 1. | Mean | 8.34 | 6.53 | 1.81 |
| 2. | S.D | 6.84 | 5.75 | 1.58 |
| 3. | C.V (%) | 82.01 | 88.05 | 87.29 |

*Source:* Computed data.

The above table exhibits the fact that the average amount of demand, collection and overdue were Rs. 8.34 lakhs, Rs. 6.53 lakhs and Rs. 1.81 lakhs respectively. The computed data shows that the coefficient of variation was high in collection. The variation is less in demand than in overdue.

The following Table 6.34 presents the trend coefficients of demand, collection and overdue of government-sponsored schemes in Union Bank of India in Kanyakumari district.

**Table 6.34: Trend and Growth of Demand, Collection and Overdue of Union Bank of India, Kanyakumari District**

| Sl. No. | Particulars | Trend Co-efficient | | | CGR (%) |
|---|---|---|---|---|---|
| | | a | b | $\overline{R}^2$ | |
| 1. | Demand | 1.76 | 0.14* (13.96) | 0.97 | 13.08 |
| 2. | Collection | 1.31 | 0.19* (12.73) | 0.97 | 17.81 |
| 3. | Overdue | 0.82 | -0.05 (-0.08) | 0.15 | -0.42 |

*Source:* Computed data. (Figures in the parentheses are t -value)

*Note:* *Indicates that the trend co-efficient are statistically significant at 5 per cent level.

The above table shows that the compound growth rates for demand and collection were 13.08 per cent and 17.81 per cent respectively. Negative growth rate of -0.42 per cent was observed in overdue. The trend coefficient shows an increase of 0.14 per cent in demand and 0.19 per cent in collection. It was negative in overdue (-0.05%).

The recovery performance of Tamilnadu Mercantile Bank in respect of government-sponsored programmes is depicted in the following Table 6.35.

Table 6.35 reveals that the Tamilnadu Mercantile Bank, a private sector bank, shows a demand position of Rs. 815.30 lakhs in its lendings, towards government-sponsored programmes under the Lead Bank Scheme during the study period. Its recovery position reveals an impressive limit of above 88 per cent during each year of study. The highest recovery limit was 98.55 per cent, achieved during the year 2000-01. The overall recovery position during the period of study was 93.18 per cent.

**Table 6.35: Recovery Performance of Tamilnadu Mercantile Bank (TMB) during the Period from 1999-2000 to 2008-09**

(*Rs. in Lakhs*)

| Sl. No. | Year | Demand | Collection | Recovery Percentage | Overdue | Overdue Percentage |
|---|---|---|---|---|---|---|
| 1. | 1999-2000 | 28.52 | 27.02 | 94.74 | 1.50 | 5.26 |
| 2. | 2000-2001 | 31.16 | 30.71 | 98.55 | 0.45 | 1.44 |
| 3. | 2001-2002 | 28.76 | 27.85 | 96.84 | 0.91 | 3.16 |
| 4. | 2002-2003 | 35.90 | 32.09 | 89.39 | 3.81 | 10.61 |
| 5. | 2003-2004 | 40.25 | 38.41 | 95.43 | 1.84 | 4.57 |
| 6. | 2004-2005 | 54.28 | 51.16 | 94.25 | 3.12 | 5.75 |
| 7. | 2005-2006 | 109.59 | 106.81 | 97.46 | 2.78 | 2.54 |
| 8. | 2006-2007 | 136.97 | 128.55 | 93.85 | 8.42 | 6.15 |
| 9. | 2007-2008 | 162.48 | 151.20 | 93.06 | 11.28 | 6.94 |
| 10. | 2008-2009 | 187.39 | 165.90 | 88.53 | 21.49 | 11.47 |
| | **Overall** | **815.30** | **759.70** | **93.18** | **55.60** | **6.82** |

*Source:* Compiled from the Annual Credit plan of IOB, Kanyakumari District, (Lead Bank) from 1999-2000 to 2008-2009.

The overdue was 1.44 per cent during 2000-01, which was the lowest. The computed data shows that the overall overdue position was 6.82 per cent during the study period.

The following Table 6.36 presents the average and stability of demand, collection and overdue of government-sponsored scheme in Tamilnadu Mercantile Bank in Kanyakumari district.

The Table 6.36 brings to light that the average amount of demand, collection and overdue were Rs. 81.53 lakhs, Rs. 75.97 lakhs and Rs. 5.56 lakhs respectively. It is observed from the results that the fluctuation was high in demand. It stood at 75.70 per cent. The coefficient of variation shows less fluctuation in 'demand' and 'overdue'.

**Table 6.36: Average and Stability of Demand, Collection and Overdue of Tamilnadu Mercantile Bank in Kanyakumari District During the Period from 1999-2000 to 2008-09**

**(*Rs. in Lakhs*)**

| Sl. No. | Particulars | Demand | Collection | Overdue |
|---|---|---|---|---|
| 1. | Mean | 81.53 | 75.97 | 5.56 |
| 2. | S.D | 61.72 | 48.98 | 6.58 |
| 3. | C.V (%) | 75.70 | 64.47 | 18.35 |

*Source:* Computed data.

The computed results of trend and growth rates in demand, collection and overdue of Tamilnadu Mercantile Bank in Kanyakumari district are given in Table 6.37.

**Table 6.37: Trend and Growth of Demand, Collection and Overdue of Tamilnadu Mercantile Bank, Kanyakumari district**

| Sl. No. | Particulars | Trend Co-efficient | | | CGR (%) |
|---|---|---|---|---|---|
| | | a | b | $\overline{R}^2$ | |
| 1. | Demand | 2.61 | 0.06* (6.32) | 0.83 | 5.14 |
| 2. | Collection | 2.52 | 0.05* (4.99) | 0.77 | 4.31 |
| 3. | Overdue | -0.46 | 0.15* (2.18) | 0.33 | 16.21 |

*Source:* Computed data. (Figures in the parentheses are t-value)

*Note:* *Indicates that the trend co-efficient are statistically significant at 5 per cent level.

It is revealed from the results that the trend coefficient has increased by 0.06 per cent for demand, 0.05 per cent for collection and 0.15 per cent for overdue. The demand, collection and overdue are statistically significant at 5 per cent level. It is observed that the growth rate was the highest in overdue. It is followed by demand and collection.

It is inferred from Table 6.38 that the overall recovery performance of Tamilnadu Mercantile Bank was 93.18 per cent. It stood first among the selected six banks followed by Indian Overseas Bank with the rate of 91.70 per cent. The State Bank of India shows 77.17 per cent recovery rate which is the lowest among the selected banks.

**Table 6.38: Ranking of Overall Recovery Performance of the Selected Banks During the Period from 1999-2000 to 2008-09**

| Sl. No. | Name of the Bank | Recovery Percentage | Rank | Overdue Percentage |
|---|---|---|---|---|
| 1. | Tamilnadu Mercantile Bank | 93.18 | I | 6.82 |
| 2. | Indian Overseas Bank | 91.70 | II | 8.30 |
| 3. | Indian Bank | 87.75 | III | 12.24 |
| 4. | Canara Bank | 84.58 | IV | 15.42 |
| 5. | Central Bank of India | 78.28 | V | 21.72 |
| 6. | State Bank of India | 77.17 | VI | 22.83 |

*Source:* Computed data.

The overdue among the selected six, banks falls between 6.82 per cent and 22.83 per cent. The overdue was found to be the highest in State Bank of India and the lowest in Tamilnadu Mercantile Bank.

The overall recovery performance in commercial banks is found to be satisfactory.

## OVERDUES AND THEIR REASONS

The overdues were to the tune of 22.83 per cent in State Bank of India, 21.72 per cent in Central Bank of India and 15.42 per cent in Canara Bank in Kanyakumari district.

Many are the reasons for the overdues. *First,* 50 per cent of the beneficiaries were not given the actual loan amount asked by them to start the units. They are, therefore, compelled to borrow from other sources, at a higher rate of interest. This exorbitant rate of interest affects the repayment performance of the beneficiaries.

*Second,* the poor repayment is attributed to severe competition in business, lack of demand for their products, and scanty demand for their products except in a particular season.

*Third,* steep hike in the prices of essential commodities has forced the beneficiaries to shell out a large sum for purchasing essential things.

*Fourth,* unforeseen domestic expenditure has led to the disposal of the units without the knowledge of the bankers.

*Fifth,* there has been a mismatch between the expected income and the actual income and hence their inability to repay the loan.

*Finally,* the beneficiaries are not able to repay the loan as they incur heavy losses caused by fire, accident and pilferage.

## VIEWS OF BANKERS AND BENEFICIARIES

### Views of Bankers

The successful functioning of the scheme depends on the effective functioning of the staff at the branch level. Since the implementation of the scheme is vested with the bankers, it would be appropriate to elicit the opinions of the bank officials, who are participating in the scheme. With a view to eliciting their opinions the Branch Managers and Field Officers of the selected bank branches in Kanyakumari district, were interviewed orally and their opinions are given under the following heads:

1. Identification of beneficiaries;
2. Time taken for disposal;
3. Reasons for rejection;
4. Experience in other schemes;
5. Reasons for overdue;
6. SC/ST target;
7. Problems experienced.

## 1. Identification of beneficiaries

Majority of the Bank Managers were of the opinion that the present system of selection of candidates by the task force at the DRDA was unsatisfactory. Loans were sanctioned mainly to achieve their fiscal targets, unmindful of the fiscal viability of the selected projects. Moreover, as a large number of candidates have to be interviewed on a particular day, time was not available for a detailed assessment of the entrepreneurial skill and the project viability. Some Managers were of the opinion that the banks should be entrusted with the selection of the candidates.

Another area, where the bankers wanted immediate improvement, was in the selection of candidates by the task force headed by the Project Officer of the DRDA in which bankers also had representation. They opined that at present the task force committee was able to spend hardly a few minutes in interviewing each candidate, because of the large number of persons to be screened in a day. This did not help them to understand their background, aptitude and integrity. One suggestion was that the task force committee could fix the target for individual banks and leave the actual selection of candidates to the banks concerned[1].

## 2. Time taken for disposal

The Managers were of the opinion that there was no delay in sanctioning and disbursing funds, as both take place simultaneously. There was a delay in the selection of candidates approaching the bank, and in the submission of required documents like quotation for purchase of assets and obtaining license. Often Field Officers were unable to make immediate spot verification.

1. Self-employment Loan—Bankers Problem, *The Hindu*, Madurai, December, 5, 1986, p. 20.

## 3. Reasons for rejection

It was reported by majority of the Branch Managers that nearly 40 per cent of the applications were rejected. The main reasons given for the rejection were as follows:

(a) Failure of the party to turn up in time

(b) Incorrect address furnished by the applicants

(c) Already employed

(d) Non-viability of the project

(e) The income of the beneficiary exceeds the stipulated income

## 4. Experience in other schemes

Regarding the Managers' experience in dealing with normal loans as compared to SGSY loans, their unanimous opinion was that recovery was comparatively easier in small loans than in SGSY loans. In the case of normal loans, reliability of the borrowers was already known since they were account holders in their banks. They unanimously declared that SGSY scheme was the most difficult scheme to implement, in terms of recovery.

## 5. Reasons for overdue

The following reasons were given for the overdue:

(a) Money spent on consumption;

(b) Willful default of the beneficiaries;

(c) Insufficient income from the projects;

(d) Indifference of the borrowers towards repayment of government loans;

(e) Non-utilization of the loan for the approved scheme;

(f) Insufficiency of loan sanctioned;

(g) Burden of repayment of loan raised from other sources to cover the deficit; and

(h) Unforeseen problems like unfavourable market situation, escalation of cost of production, power-cuts, non-availability of raw materials.

Most of the Bank Managers were of the opinion that, wilful default and indifference to repayment of government loans are the most important reasons for the mounting overdues.

## 6. Scheduled caste and scheduled tribe target

The Branch Managers were of the opinion that they were unable to achieve the target set in the schemes meant for the SC/ST owing to the following reasons:

*(a)* Lack of genuine demand from them;

*(b)* Lack of entrepreneurship;

*(c)* Attachment to traditional occupation;

*(d)* Preference to avail credit under other schemes where subsidy is as much as 50 percent (THADCO); and

*(e)* Preference for wage employment to self-employment.

## 7. Problems experienced

The major problem confronting the Managers was the lack of personnel to supervise this and other schemes. This scheme requires frequent field visits and the field officers are unable to contact the beneficiaries as often as it necessary. The Managers unanimously hold the view that there is a need for personal collateral security at the time of issue of loans and necessity for bringing in legal safeguards.

## Views of Beneficiaries

The views expressed by the beneficiaries, on the government sponsored schemes are given below:

Almost all the beneficiaries welcome the schemes as they provide them with the finance necessary to start a venture on their own and at the same time have expressed the need for suitable modification in the schemes to make them effective.

The general opinion of the beneficiaries was that payment of interest on loan could be postponed till the lapse of the moratorium period fixed by the Bank. As per the scheme, the beneficiaries have to pay interest from the date of disbursement of the loan. The time lag involved in the generation of income from the commissioned project has made the repayment of the loan with interest, a difficult task for the borrowers. Beneficiaries at large were ignorant of the role of DRDA and its single window concept for assisting small entrepreneurs. The sample beneficiaries were not aware of the assistance they had received from DRDA and they only knew DRDA as a place for interview and selection. Therefore, it was suggested that a special cell be started in banks, essentially, to scrutinize the applications and render necessary technical assistance.

The prevailing rate of interest of 10 per cent for backward areas and 12 per cent for other places is considered to be high by the sample beneficiaries. It was also suggested that interest free loans may be given instead of subsidy.

Some of the sample beneficiaries were of the opinion that the moratorium period given, is too short and there was a dissatisfied feeling that the repayment starts immediately after the receipt of loan.

Some of the sample beneficiaries have accused the bank personnels for unnecessarily reducing the loan amount recommended by DRDA.

7

# Summary of Findings Suggestions and Conclusion

## INTRODUCTION

As per the Reserve Bank of India (RBI) guidelines, 10 per cent of the advance in the total lending by a Commercial Bank, should go to the Government-sponsored employment schemes. The loans sanctioned under these programmes come under priority sector lending. The bank credits for these programmes are included in the District Credit Plan. But lack of financial assets such as credit and savings stultifies the entrepreneurial ventures. With a view to circumventing this bottleneck, the innovative arrangement for the proper financial credit through commercial bank came into being. The present study is an attempt to analyse commercial bank advances under the Lead Bank Scheme and evaluate the government-sponsored employment scheme in Kanyakumari district.

The trend and growth of lending under the Lead Bank Scheme, evaluation of Lead Bank Scheme, in terms of growth and equity with block-wise comparison and evaluation of Government-sponsored programmes under the Lead Bank Scheme in Kanyakumari district have been discussed. The findings of the investigator, based on the discussion and analyses are recounted. Suggestions for the successful implementation of the schemes, plugging the loopholes in the process of implementation are also offered. The investigator firmly believes that the suggestions, if accepted and carried out in earnest, will yield rich dividends.

## SUMMARY OF FINDINGS

The investigator has found an increase in the number of the branches of the commercial banks under Lead Bank that are associated with the implementation of the schemes sponsored by the Government. The 147 branches in 1999-2000 shot up to 174 branches in 2008-09. The trend coefficient shows that the advance amount has also increased at the rate of 0.124. The deposits made by commercial banks under Lead Bank Schemes was less than the advances.

The share of government-sponsored schemes has increased by 0.025 per cent. Similarly, the share of advances to priority sector has increased by 0.074 per cent during the period of study. The compound growth rate of advances to all sectors, government-sponsored scheme and priority sector has registered an upward trend of 13.25 per cent, 2.56 per cent and 7.68 per cent respectively. The lowest trend was observed in advances to government-sponsored schemes by commercial banks under Lead Bank Schemes than advances to priority sector. The actual advances to government-sponsored programmes were found to be less than the target amount. The significant and positive trend and growth rates were observed both in target as well as actual amounts.

The outstanding advances in government-sponsored schemes to total advances has shown a fluctuating trend. The trend rates were 0.042 per cent, 0.068 per cent and 0.029 per cent per annum for total advances, priority sector advances and government-sponsored scheme advances respectively. The outstanding advances to priority sector were highly fluctuating compared to government-sponsored programmes. The trend and growth of outstanding in total advances, priority sector and government-sponsored programmes were statistically significant and positive.

The analysis casts light on the recovery position. The rate of recovery ranged from 64 per cent in 2000-01 to 87 per cent in 2007-08. The demand has less fluctuation followed by collection when compared to overdue during the period of study. Trend and growth were positive and significant as far as collection was concerned, whereas they were found to be significant and negative as far as overdue is concerned.

As to the performance of various blocks, the analysis underscores the fact that Killiyoor, Kurunthencode, Munchirai, Rajakkamangalam and Thiruvattar had registered higher overall growth rate in the disbursement of amount under SJSRY Scheme. With regard to the SGSY scheme, Kurunthencode, Munchirai, Rajakkamangalam and Thiruvattar have had high growth in the allocation of funds by commercial banks under Lead Bank Scheme. The overall growth rate of the PMRY scheme was higher in Killiyoor, Munchirai, Rajakkamangalam and Thiruvattar blocks. In the case of TAHDCO, Munchirai, Rajakkamangalam and Thovalai have registered higher overall growth rate in the allocation of funds by the commercial banks under Lead Bank Scheme.

The classification analysis revealed that Rajakkamangalam ranks first in the allocation of funds in all four schemes. The pattern and measure revealed that Rajakkamangalam is the first in all four government-sponsored programmes under Lead Bank Scheme and Thuckalay the last in all schemes. The other blocks fall in between. The equity analysis showed that Rajakkamangalam is the model block for all other blocks in Kanyakumari district. The Agasteeswaram block had the distinction of achieving more than the target in SGSY and TAHDCO schemes. This study makes it clear that there was inequity in the allocation of funds to all the four schemes among the blocks except Rajakkamangalam.

It has been found that more than 47 per cent of the respondents belong to the age group of 30-40 years in both sectors in the study area. Nearly 60 per cent are male beneficiaries. It has been observed that the sample beneficiaries are well educated and more than 90 per cent of them are graduates, post-graduates and possessed technical qualifications in non-agricultural sector. In the case of agricultural sector, nearly 46 per cent are found to be upto S.S.L.C. 90 per cent of them are married in both agricultural and non-agricultural sectors.

Out of 300 beneficiaries, more than 50 per cent belong to BC/MBC category. Christians are found to be more in agriculture and allied activities sector.

Regarding the family size, majority of them are having families with 3-5 members. More than 75 per cent are living in joint family.

Further, it has been observed that majority of the beneficiaries' monthly income falls in the category of Rs. 5000-10000 in both the sectors. Majority of the respondents are getting loan for the reason 'lack of employment opportunities' in both sectors. Majority of the beneficiaries have got information from 'friends/relatives' and 'voluntary organisation'. 'Influence of the training' is the foremost reason for the beneficiaries to choose the present venture in agriculture and allied sectors. Majority of the respondents prepared the project report, 'by others on the basis of suggestions given by the beneficiary'.

Regarding the asset position, it was found that after availing loans under government-sponsored schemes, the position of the beneficiaries under the asset group of Rs. 20,000 to 30,000 has improved and it is followed by the asset group whose income is below Rs. 20, 000. The sector wise increase in asset position was found to be the highest in non-agricultural sector.

Regarding employment generation, the average mandays generated among the family members and hired hands have been found to be the highest in the income group whose per capita income ranged from Rs. 2000 to Rs. 4000. Sector-wise, the non-agricultural sector has provided more number of mandays both within the family and hired labourers.

Regarding the identification of the factors which influence the repayment of loans, the loan amount received and the installments had significant effects on the repayment of loan under government-sponsored schemes.

It is ascertained from the analysis that the trend coefficient was positive in demand and collection in all the six banks selected for the study. It reveals the increasing trend in the disbursement of loan and encouraging trend in the collection of loan instalments. It is observed that the compound growth rate of demand and collection was found positive in all banks.

The recovery has been found to be the best in Tamilnadu Mercantile Bank among the selected banks. IOB is the Lead Bank in Kanyakumari district, which ranked second in recovery with 91.70 per cent. The overall recovery has been satisfactory with more than 77.17 per cent in all six banks selected for the study.

## SUGGESTIONS

For increasing the advances made by the commercial banks and for better implementation of various schemes the following suggestions are offered:

Whenever the government launches schemes for the upliftment of the marginalized people, it is the people who are well-off, jump to their feet. They manage to have the lion's share by hook or nook. As a result, the people who are really in need of financial help are pushed aside. Unscrupulous politicians have a hand in it. They force the bank officials to sanction loans to the people who are known to them. To cap it all, they advise the loanees not to repay the loan amount periodically. They have a strong belief that the loans will be waived at some time or the other, especially, just before the general election. This attitude is detrimental to the success of the schemes. It will be better of the politicians clear the field and give way to the needy people.

The bank officials should have a say whenever new schemes are introduced. They should be given an opportunity to study the feasibility and viability of the schemes. The government should try to implement the schemes only after the green signal is given by the bank officials.

In spite of their best efforts, the bankers find it difficult to know correctly the background of the applicants. Sometimes, false addresses are given and their existing employment is concealed by the applicants. One way of overcoming these difficulties would be to inspect the ration card of the applicant and to demand the recommendations of at least two account holders, well known to the particular bank branch. This is needed since the scheme does not provide for collateral security or third party guarantee.

In order to improve the repayment level of the loan amount, the subsidy amount should be linked to the prompt repayment of the loan. The honest repayers may be encouraged by offering more subsidies. At the same time, the amount of subsidy should be reduced to the defaulters. Under no circumstances should any subsidy be given to the wilful defaulters. This will have a stimulating effect on the wilful defaulters.

While processing the applications for loans, the bank officials should look into the real needs of the applicants. Those who need really more must be given more. They should not be given less. At the same time, those who do not really need should not be given what they ask for. If the former is given less or if the latter is given more, it will not only impair the success of the schemes but also affect the recovery of the loan.

Instead of giving loans to individuals, the government may explore the possibility of giving loans to joint ventures of the youth. To begin with, one or two joint ventures may be selected and provided with loans in every block.

A few of the blocks are big and hence unwieldy. The investigator suggests that such enormous blocks be bifurcated for the successful implementation of the schemes.

## CONCLUSION

The researcher is able to move up to this concluding section after mopping up of resourceful inputs relating to the subject chosen for this research study. It is also with a sense of satisfaction since a local problem has been researched by employing the art and science of investigation at the micro and macro levels, well within the scope of the study. Though a few problems and areas may be a little insignificant, the synthetic, analytical framework has been kept alive and intact throughout the process of throwing light.

Certain technical and human biases based on difficulties of retrieval and recall might have crept in but they have been suitably neutralised and held at the safe limits, in order to achieve objective observation of facts. The chapters containing analytical frames and logical illustrations as well as inference, enjoy the required sequential stamina and stress. This makes this work a little than so far tried claims.

On the basis of the data analysed and interpreted one is able to understand the degree of objectivity and thoroughness with which the bank officials function and achieve. They deserve special mention in this context. Educating the common masses in banking activities needs lot of courage and confidence, which are strengthened by the nature of co-operation extended by the beneficiaries. They work and serve with skill and will. Still a few areas evade inspection and introspection.

In fine, it can be humbly felt that this fact-finding exercise has proved to be an academic joy and valuable addition to the fund of rewarding knowledge in this area. One can become highly optimistic that the suggestions advanced in this study are bound to pave the way for greater success.

## SCOPE FOR FURTHER RESEARCH

This work provides potentiality and scientific scope for further research in many areas. The following areas are a few to name:

1. A study on the Performance evaluation of priority sector lending in Kanyakumari district.
2. A comparative study of the Lead Bank Schemes in Kanyakumari District with other districts.
3. A study of Lead Bank Scheme-Sector-wise analysis in Kanyakumari district.

# Bibliography

## Books

Bhattacharya, D., *"Concise History of Indian Economy"*, Hall of India Pvt.Ltd., New Delhi, 1989.

Chandra Sekar, K., *"History of Banking"*, Deep & Deep Publication, New Delhi, 1995.

Dandekar, V.M., *"The Indian Economy 1947-1992, Agriculture"*, Sage Publication, New Delhi, 1994.

Ghosal, S.N., *"Agricultural Financing in India"*, Asia Publishing House, Bombay, 1972.

Gorden and Natarajan, *"Banking Theory Law and Practice"*, Himalaya Publishing House, Bombay, 1995.

Hamumantha Rao, C.H., "Policy Issues, Relating to Irrigation and Rural Credit in G.S. Bhallq (ed) *"Economic Liberalisation and Indian Agriculture"*, Institution for Studies in Industrial Development 1994.

Hopkin, J.A., Barry, P.G. and Baker, C.B., *"Financial Management in Agriculture"*, Interstate Printer and Publisher Inc., New York, 1973

Joshi, P.L., *"Institutional Financing in India"*, Deep and Deep Publication, New Delhi, 1985.

Keshekhar, *"Banking Theory, Law and Practice"*, Vikas Publishing House, New Delhi, 1997.

Maheshwari, S.N., "*Banking Law and Practice*", Kalyani Publishers, Ludhiana, 1996.

Manickam, S., "*Economic Development of Tamil Nadu in Perspective*", Uyrimmai Publications, Chennai, 2006.

Nand Kishore Jha, N., "*Bank Finance and Green Revolution in India*", Amar Prakashan Publication, New Delhi, 1985.

Natarajan, S. and Parameswaran, R., "*Indian Banking*", Sultan Chand & Company Ltd., New Delhi, 2001.

Reena Verma, "*Poverty and Poverty Alleviation Programmes*", Spectrum Hand Book of General Studies Spectrum Book of Publishers Ltd., 2003

Shahidur S.R. Khandker, "*Fighting Poverty with Micro Credit: Experience in Bangladesh*", Oxford University Press, New York, 1988.

Singh, C.P., "*Poverty Alleviation Programmes Under the Plans*", Indian Publishing Company, New Delhi, 1980.

Sipra Dasgupta, T., "*Class Relations and Technical Changes in Indian Agriculture*", Institute of Economic Growth, New Delhi, 1980.

Subramanian, K., and Velayudham, T.K., *Banking Reforms in India*, Tata McGraw Hill Publishing Company Ltd., 1997.

Tanton, T.N., "*Banking Theory Law and Practice in India*", Indian Law House, Delhi, 2005.

Tara Chand, "*Policies of Poverty Alleviation, General Studies for UPSC Civil Servant, Preliminary Examination*", Tata McGraw Hills Winning Edge Series, 2003.

Vasant Desai, "*Indian Banking Nature and Problems*", Himalaya Publishing House, Bombay, 1980.

**Journals**

Acharya, T.K.T., Dhogade, M.C. and Lopes, M.M., "A Study of Credit Problems of Farmers in a Tribal Area of Maharashtra", *Agriculture and Agro-Industries Journal*, Vol. 5, February, 1992.

Agarwal, M.L. and Kumawat, R.K., *"Potentialities of Increasing Farm Income through Credit and New Technology"*, Agricultural Situation in India, Vol. 28, No. 9, 1974.

Amarjit Kahlon, R., "Development Oriented Service area approach of Bank Branches", *National Bank News Review*, June-August, 1990.

Anthony Bottomley, "Interest Rate Determining in Underdeveloped Rural Areas", *American Journal of Agricultural Economics*, Vol. 57, No. 2, May 1975.

Atiqur Rahman, T., "Usury Capital and Credit Relations in Bangladesh Agriculture: Some Implications for Capital Formation and Capitalist Growth", *Bangladesh Development Studies*, Vol. 7, No. 2, 1997.

Bhargava, V.K. and Shah, S.L., "A Study of Credit Requirements and Advances to Farmers in Patiala District", *Indian Journal of Agricultural Economics*, Vol. 23, No. 3, 1986.

Chandrasekar, D.K., "Commercial Banking in Tamilnadu: An Overview", *Southern Economist*, Vol. 23, December 1988.

Chitranjan, "Credit Rationing—A Perspective", *Financing Agriculture*, Vol. 18, No. 324, July-December, 1986.

Chowdhery, P., "Farm Credit Needs and the Role of Commercial Banks to Financing". *Indian Journal of Agricultural Economics*, Vol. 23, No. 3, 1968.

Desai, D.K., "Institutional Credit Requirements for Agricultural Production in 2000 A.D.", *Indian Journal of Agricultural Economics*, Vol. XLIII, No. 3, July-December, 1988.

Dra Srivastava, D.H., Sirohi, A.S., Singh, D. and Singh, K.N., "Analysis of Productive Use of Credit in I.R.D.P. Shabad, Bombay", *Financing Agriculture*, Vol. 2, No. 2, 1970.

Erappa, S., "IRDP Experience of SC/ST in Karnataka", *Southern Economist*, Vol. 33, No. 20, 1995.

Johl, S.S. and Singh, B.P., "An Evaluation of Agricultural and Co-operative Credit in Punjab", *Indian Co-operative Review*, 1965.

Karan Singh and Ashwanikumar Garg, "Impact of Small Farmers Development Agencies on Its Beneficiaries in Punjab", *Financing Agriculture*, Vol. 7, No. 3, 1975.

Kulsherestha, U.C., "Lead Banks — Restropect and Prospects", *Journal of Indian Institute of Bankers*, October-December, Vol. 56, No. 4, 232, 1985.

Kulwant Singh, "Co-operative Agricultural Credit Utilisation in Himachal Pradesh", *Finance India*, Vol. 10, No. 3, September, 1996.

Laxmi Narayanan, H., "Poverty Alleviation — Where has IRDP gone Wrong?", *Economic Times*, 1986.

Mahalingam, N., "Bank Credit for Economic Development", *Kisan World*, Vol. 32, No. 7, July 2005.

Mahendra D., Desai and Bharat D. Naik., "Prospects of Demand for Short-Term Institutional Credit for High Yielding Varieties", *Indian Journal of Agricultural Economics*, Vol. 26, No. 4, October-December, 1971.

Margarete Berger, N., "Giving Women Credit: The Strengths and Limitations of Credit as a Tool for Alleviating Poverty", *World Development*, Vol. 17, No. 7, 1989.

Meenashi Anand Chandhary., "Empowering Strategies for Rural Women in India", *Kurukshatra*, Vol. XLIV, No. 6, 1996.

Melichar Emmanual, K., "Farm Credit: On Credit Projections", *Indian Journal of Agricultural Economics*, Vol. 24, No. 4, 1984.

Mitra, S. and Lahiri, D., "Expectations from Co-operatives Belied or Misplaced", *Indian Co-operative Review*, Vol. 1, 1996.

Mohan Rao, J., "Interest Rates in Backward Agriculture", *Cambridge Journal of Economics*, Vol. 4, 1980.

Namasivayam, D., "NREP in Tamil Nadu: Comparison of Growth and Equality by Taxonomic Method", *Margin*, October-December 1987.

Nicholson, R., "Report Regarding the Possibility of Introducing Agricultural Banks in Madras State", *Reserve Bank of India*, Vol. 1, No. 1, 1960.

Pallavi Chavan and Ram Kumar, "Micro Credit and Rural Poverty: An analysis of Empirical Evidence", *Economic and Political Weekly*, Vol. XXXVII, No. 10, 2002.

Pandy, H.K., "Credit Need in Changing Agriculture", *Financing Agriculture*, Vol. 4, No. 1, 1973.

Parameswaran Iyer, K., "Creating Rural Employment — JRYS New Thrust Area", *Economic and Political Weekly*, Vol. 21(32), 1994.

Pothulum, C. and Someshwar, K., "Labour Absorption Through IRDP", *Rural India*, Vol.13, October-November, 1992.

Pranab Bardhan, L. and Ashok Rudra, K., "Interlinkages of Land, Labour and Credit Relations: An Analysis of Village Survey Data in East India", *Economic and Political Weekly*, Vol. 13, February 1993.

Prasad, H., "Employment and Income in Rural India", *Economic and Political Weekly*, Vol. 7, No. 2, 1986.

Rajagopalan, V., "Farm Liquidity and Institutional Financing for Agricultural Development", *Indian Journal of Agriculture Economics*, Vol. 23, No. 4, 1968.

Ramadass, M., "Demand for and Productivity of Farm Credit in Pondicherry Region", *Economic Appraisal*, 1998.

Ruddar Datt, "Jawahar Rozgar Yojana — A Review", *Southern Economists*, Vol. 34, No. 10, 1995.

Sain, K., "Role of Co-operative in Green Revolution — A Movement for Contemplation", *Indian Co-operative Review*, Vol. 11, No. 2, January 1994.

Sankarama, R., "Pattern of Values of Rural Co-operative Leaders in India", *Institute of Rural Management*, Vol.17, No.3, 1996.

Sharma, J.S. and Prasad, B., "An Assessment of Production Credit Needs in Developing Agriculture", *Indian Journal of Agricultural Economics*, Vol. 26, No. 4, October-December, 1971.

Shukla, B.D. and Misra, S.D., "Impact of Co-operative Finance — A Case Study in a Block of Uttar Pradesh", *Financing Agriculture*, Vol. 6, No. 2, 1996.

Singh, G.N., Azad Rajeeva Srivastava, M.P. and Gupta, B.R., "Role of Land Development Bank in Raising Production, Productivity and Income in Agriculture", *Indian Co-operative Review*, Vol. 17, No. 3, 1980.

Singh, R.K.P. and Upadhayaya, K.M., "A Study of Loan Recovery of Regional Rural Bank in Bihar", *Finance Agriculture*, Vol. 16, No. 2, 2002.

Srivastava, K., "Estimation of Credit for Agriculture", *Financing Agriculture*, Vol. 4, No. 1, 1996.

Subramanian, R., "Impact Bank Credit and Technology on Net Return of Farmers in Coimbatore Taluk, Tamil Nadu", *Mysore Journal of Agricultural Science*, Vol. 10, No. 3, 1996.

Subramaniyan, K.V. and Patel, R.K., "Impact of Capital Availability on Farm Income and Demand for Short Term Credit in West Godavari District, Andhra Pradesh", *Agricultural Situation in India*, Vol. 28, No. 3, 1983.

Sydney Ruth Schuler, Hashemi, S.M. and Riley, A.P., "The Influence of Women's Charging Roles and Status in Bangladesh Fertility Transition: Evidence from a Study of Credit Programmes in Contraceptive Use", *World Development*, Vol. 25, No. 4, 1997.

Vashisht, S.K., "Distribution and Utilisation of Short-term Co-operative Credit on Hoshiapur District of Punjab", *Indian Co-operative Review*, Vol. XVIII, No. 3, April 1981.

Yadava, J.P., Ramachandra and Pandey, S.P., "Small Farmers and Their Credit Requirement: Its Availability and Sources"; *Indian Co-operative Review*, Vol. 7, No. 3, 1975.

## Reports

*Annual Credit Plan*, Published by Lead Bank Section of IOB, Kanyakumari District, 1999-2000 to 2008-09.

*Economic Appraisal 2002-03*, Evaluation and Applied Research Department, Government of Tamil Nadu, Chennai.

Reserve Bank of India, *All India Debt and Investment Survey*, 1971-72.

Reserve Bank of India, *Functions and Workings*, 5th Edition.

Rural Labour Enquiry Committee, 1974-75, *Final Report on Indebtedness Among Rural Labour Households*, December 18, 1978.

*Tamilnadu—An Economic Appraisal*, Evaluation of Applied Research Department, Government of Tamil Nadu, Chennai, 2002-03.

## Thesis

Balram Sahar, *A Study on Repayment of Dairy Loans Financed Under IRDP (Goraul Block, Muzaffarpur District)*, Unpublished Thesis, Department of Agricultural Economics, RAO, Bihar, 2000.

Gokhale, H.V. "*A Study of Bank of India as Lead Bank in Chandrapur District with Special Emphasis on Priority Sector*", Unpublished Thesis, Nagpur University, Nagpur, 1990.

Subha Rao, B. "*Study of Commercial Bank Finance to Agriculture in Prakasam District—Andhra Pradesh*", Unpublished Thesis, Banaras Hindu University. 1990.

# Index

## F



## G



## H



## I

**J**



**K**



**L**



**M**